Sound Health
Sound Wealth

The Biology of
Hope & Manifestation

Luanne Oakes, Ph.D.

Nightingale-Conant

Sound Health, Sound Wealth

What people are saying about
Dr. Luanne Oakes and
Sound Health, Sound Wealth:

"Dr. Luanne Oakes navigates the human condition with unique and refreshing brilliance. Her writing and music is the product of intellect, intuition, education, experience, and compassion. I have had the splendid opportunity to work with Dr. Luanne Oakes and I know the following to be true. ... She assists you in calling forth your higher self; she aides your personal development, all with gentle but radiant energy and unmatched skill. Unequivocally, Dr. Luanne Oakes has enhanced my life and my living of it."

– LYNNE SIMONS,
Court Master, Second Judicial District Court, Reno, Nevada

"The *Sound Health, Sound Wealth* Frequency Treatment™ CD, by Luanne Oakes, Ph.D., helps you achieve a state of profound relaxation. I think everyone can benefit from it."

– DEEPAK CHOPRA, M.D.,
Author, *Ageless Body, Timeless Mind*

"*Sound Health, Sound Wealth* ... is an integrative blend of scientific wisdom and the healing arts that promotes

well-being and accelerates expansion of the whole
self through sound-frequency technology."

— JOHN GRAY, Ph.D.,
Author, *Men Are from Mars, Women Are from Venus*

"*In Sound Health, Sound Wealth,* Luanne Oakes, Ph.D.,
masterfully blends ancient spiritual truth with
whole-brain learning."

— REV. MARY MURRAY SHELTON,
Author, *Guidance from the Darkness*

" I met Dr. Luanne Oakes when I was in a serious
physical and emotional crisis. She has restored my
physical health. Her radiance and loving compassion have awakened me to a new peacefulness, a
deepening imagination and smiles. I never knew
such change was possible. My heart is filled with
love and gratitude."

— MRS. JANE FELLMAN,
Social Activist and Specialist in
Deep Forgiveness and Social Change

" Luanne has been such a bright light in my life.
Through her infinite wisdom and radiant love I was
able to find the golden key that unlocked a lifetime
of difficult issues regarding my weight. My life has

been transformed. I now have a new and wondrous relationship with food and I am effortlessly maintaining my desired weight. My heart is filled with love and gratitude."

— KRISTIN LEWANDOWSKI,
Retired Teacher and Educational Specialist

" After a devastating romantic breakup nearly three years ago I was left with a world of shattered dreams and few hopes of ever living in an abundant and loving life until I began listening to your ... *Sound Health Sound Wealth* CD program. My life has changed, charged with dreams again, fulfillment, and energy, opening many new facets of creating the life I wish to live. Thank You!"

— STEVE DISTROLA,
Cadillac/Range Rover Motor Car Company

" Dr. Luanne Oakes has transformed my life! She has been instrumental in illuminating my sense of inner peace, while transforming and providing me with golden keys to unlocking life's magical doors. I have abundant wealth, amazing laughter and radiant eye sparkling moments every day. My body is vibrant, my cells sing and my art is flourishing! She has given me the tools to manifest my most miraculous dreams, and all of them are coming true."

— MATT LEW
Artist

Sound Health, Sound Wealth

Library of Congress Cataloging-in-Publication Data

Oakes, Luanne.
  South health, sound wealth : the biology of hope & manifestation / Luanne Oakes.
  p. cm.

  ISBN 978-1-4243-2391-3

Printed in the United States of America.

SPECIAL ACKNOWLEDGMENTS

I would like to thank Stephanie Dillon, Ph.D., for her guidance in taking literally thousands of pages and condensing them into this shortened manuscript. You are a brilliant writer, Spiritual being, and incredible doctor of psychology.

I have tremendous gratitude to you, Dan Strutzel, Vice President of Nightingale-Conant, for your friendship, unwavering faith, and encouragement. Thank you for your brilliance, kindness, and compassion.

Special thanks to the staff at the Nightingale-Conant Corporation for asking me to write this book. I am deeply honored.

Mom, Shari, and Michael, thank you for your unwavering love and care from childhood and still now. Lily, you are a true gift in my life as well as being a fantastic artist, graphic designer, and my best friend since kindergarten. We have certainly shared much laughter, creativity, and tears over our blessedly long lifetimes.

M. Christina Benson, M.D., and Kenneth Wells, M.D., you are also "family" to me. Your love and support mean so much. Thank you, Ken, for my magical silver flute!

Love and thanks to my dear friends Steven Swinford, Joanne Shoenfield, and Bill Hunter who live, dream, and share their Magical Divine Experiences in our favorite ocean paradise.

Thank you, Theresa Puskar, who, from a cozy, beautiful timber lodge in the glow of a huge, warm fireplace, looking over beautiful Lake Tahoe and surrounded by miles of snow, outlined this book over dinner. I so appreciate all your assistance and editing of all my other Nightingale-Conant projects over the years. You are a bright and shining gem.

I have tremendous gratitude to my patients and clients, who have literally taught me how best to assist them throughout the years.

I also want to thank Mitch Sisskind for his tremendous editing skills. And, finally, much gratitude to Dr. Deepak Chopra for always being compassionately supportive of my work.

Table of Contents

Sound Health, Sound Wealth

Making a Decision

There is so much I wish to accomplish in this book. It is my dream to share as many possibilities from the widest possible perspective in regard to the physical, emotional, and Spiritual experiences of your everyday world. I realize that this is a very ambitious idea. This book is for the wonderful, miraculous clients and patients I have been so privileged to know, and also for you whom I do not yet know. This book is from my heart to yours.

My intention is to give as much assistance as I might offer through these pages and the enclosed CD for you to enjoy the very highest and best in your life always, and in all ways, as we share life's often surprising, sometimes very difficult, and wondrous journey. Everything that we will discuss in these pages will take place in the context of the Universe as a whole: the outer Universe of the galaxies, and the inner Universe of the cells, molecules, and atoms of which "you" are composed. Even further, we will also explore the non-physical, nonlinear, Spiritual Universe whose existence science is not yet able to verify — but I <u>know</u> it exists.

It has been said that each choice is a doorway to an alternate Universe. Each and every thought, choice, and action triggers another significant possibility of how our individual life experiences will unfold.

In the Spiritual Universe of my own thoughts, I have consciously *Made a Decision* to be my very highest and best in all areas of my life, to have the very best life possible, and to feel the best that I can: Body, Mind, and Spirit. I want to invite you to make that same decision, with your own unique style, so that you will enjoy more fulfillment, pleasure, and joy through Sound Health and Sound Wealth. Most importantly, we can enjoy the process, one day, one hour, one moment at a time. I know being our highest and best is a lifelong process with many mistakes along the way. However, our mistakes most often pave the way for our resounding success.

In order to bring all this about, we will of course build upon the information and stories that you'll find in these pages, as well as on your own very individual and unique life experience. Just as importantly, the CD program you'll find on the inside back cover is an instrument, or "Effortless Power Tool," for making the intention of this book come true.

Sound — with the dual meaning of fundamental strength and audio phenomena — is the basis of this book. Since listening is often the best way to access sound, I hope you will utilize and enjoy the healing audio energy of the CD as much as possible, or as often as it feels comfortable to you.

EFFORTLESS ENHANCEMENT

Making a Decision to change your thoughts also changes your life, producing the rich, illuminating experiences you want — physically, emotionally, and Spiritually. By *Making a Decision*, you <u>effortlessly enhance</u> your own internal Universe, creating an expanded self, an enriched life experience, and a better world. By *Making a Decision* for yourself, you impact the world around you; your decision is like throwing a pebble into a pond. The ripples affect and literally transform the entire Universe. What's more, you can create these extraordinary and exciting transformations without walking out your front door, without going online, without getting on a plane, and without traveling to Lourdes to be healed.

We make decisions constantly — decisions that powerfully affect the quality of our lives. Yet, we are often unaware of the decisions that float outside our conscious awareness. These subconscious decisions may significantly impact our life scripts, and our behavior, sometimes resulting in situations that are negative or painful. We may be surprised or even shocked when we experience outcomes that we never intended or consciously desired. As we become increasingly and exquisitely more aware of all our thoughts, feelings, and beliefs, conscious and subconscious, we then have the power to orchestrate and affect our own positively enriched unique experience of life.

Sound Health, Sound Wealth

As a foundational transformative ingredient of *Sound Health, Sound Wealth,* I will review with you my understanding of the power of the Subconscious Mind, as well as ways for bringing the Subconscious Mind to conscious awareness. You may then tap into the limitless power of your Subconscious Mind and use its direct connection to the *Quantum Hologram,* the Source of All, which is known by many names: Higher Power, Divine Intelligence, God, Mother Nature, the Akashic Records, or whatever name feels appropriate to you in reference to a Power Greater Than Yourself. Perhaps that power is not singular.

Dr. Carl Jung believed that when we have an inner situation or belief that we are not aware of on a conscious level, it becomes manifested or "acted out" in our behavior. It makes sense that we must uncover our subconscious beliefs that can deny us access to our highest and best selves and our dreams. For these compelling reasons, my intention for this introduction is to provide you with specific ideas and techniques that allow your subconscious thoughts, feelings, and desires to become consciously known and understood. This information makes you the master architect of your own life experience, clearing your path to create exactly what you need and desire.

In recent years, the author Earl Nightingale uncovered a mystical and scientific secret he referred to as "The Strangest Secret." As he put it, "We become what we think about most of the time." Earl Nightingale's "Strangest Secret" has been proven irrefutably correct. Ancient Wisdom and Quantum Physics alike demonstrate this.

What do <u>you</u> think about most of the time? How do you feel about your present life, your loved ones, your friendships, and your work? Do you love what you do? Do you have pleasure, enjoyment, and relaxation, each and every day? Do you live where you want to live? Are you surrounded by the particular unique environments — beauty in nature, city diversity, rejuvenating familiar rituals, spontaneous adventures — that nourish, support, and energize you? Do you feel safe and secure financially? Do you enjoy optimum health, vibrant energy, and resounding well-being? How many dreams from your childhood have materialized? What dreams do you have now?

Each and every thought has a neurochemical, biological, and molecular equivalent. Thoughts <u>do</u> become things. *Alchemy* is one term for this process of transforming one thing into something entirely different. *Sound Health, Sound Wealth* assists you in becoming your own Alchemical healer, creating the exact deeply rich life experience you so want and deserve. What's more, in the *Sound Health, Sound Wealth* Alchemical process, we fulfill our desires, not at the expense of others or of the environment.

We tend to think of Alchemy in dramatic terms, as in the transformation of lead into gold, or ashes into a rose. However, Alchemy occurs more frequently than we might think, and often very subtly. An everyday example of Alchemy occurs when you imagine biting into a lemon. Your body responds instantly, by creating the biochemistry for digestion, and you salivate at this imaginary experience. Your thought Alchemically became a thing that created a physical experience. Experiment with this idea, and you will discover for yourself how quickly a thought can become a thing.

THE DECISION FOR SOUND HEALTH AND SOUND WEALTH

How do you feel when reading the following statement?

You are enjoying a sense of radiant well-being, vibrant energy, peace, joy, fulfillment, and hope as never before. You are surrounded in loving, harmonious relationships. You are happy, joyous, and free. If you are not already, you are going to be wealthy. Very large sums of "Life Force in the form of money" are flowing into your life — enough to provide for your children and your children's children, enough to do great things in the world, for yourself and/or others. In short, any financial worries you may have had are now in the past. Our global environment and planetary concerns are being repaired and healed in an astonishing and timely fashion. A plush, rejuvenated emerald planet is now emerging using the unlimited resources available through the incredible bridging of science and Spirit.

**It sounds very positive, doesn't it?
Perhaps even a bit suspicious.**

Because it is very possible that you don't believe all or part of what you have just read. You may not believe that you will achieve radiant well-being, peace, fulfillment, joy, and hope, or even great financial success. In fact, you may not even want to achieve some or all the above-mentioned. A vast majority of people at one time or another, even now, believe that enjoying all these things, including wealth, is not possible. Many have been raised to believe that money and Spirituality are mutually exclusive. Also, that if you have more, others will have less. Daunting documented facts of planetary depletion have far exceeded publicly projected possibilities for a rejuvenated emerald planet.

But the truth is that we are living in a richly abundant Universe with unlimited resources. Wondrous, vast, scientifically Spiritual possibilities abound: from molecular computers able to hold the same information as the largest computer in the world in the size of a dime, to living biological machines that — without harm to any person, animal, place, or thing — through Alchemy, can neutralize nuclear waste into organic, viable living material. It our individual and collective choice to expand our focus and awareness of these unlimited opportunities! As the age-old adage says, "<u>What we focus on increases!</u>"

Sound Health, Sound Wealth

The purpose of this book, and the CD that accompanies it, is to offer a definition of Sound Health and Sound Wealth, to provide an array of enhancing and expanding choices, hope, and new possibilities. I would also like to assist you in discerning any beliefs, subconscious and conscious, that may he separating you from the very highest and best that you deserve: emotionally, physically, Spiritually, and even financially. I will present ideas that differentiate merely surviving, to enjoying the plenitude of Sound Health and Sound Wealth <u>you</u> so richly deserve.

Sound is the integrating factor of all life. Ancient Eastern Mystics, the Christian, Jewish, Buddhist, Islamic, and Hindu religions, as well as all other equally notable traditions, religions, and philosophies, have acknowledged that it is the vibration of "Sound" that ultimately sustains both the heavens and the earth. The word *Sound* literally means "health."

Literal definitions of the word *Sound* include "healthy," "robust," "secure financially," "reliable," "enduring of character," "upright," "honorable," and even "to seek to ascertain."

Sound and Light are different aspects of the same force. On the light scale of physics, sound and light are 40 octaves apart. It is the differentiation and fluctuations of vibrations of subatomic particles of sound and light that create each pattern that becomes human, animal, flower, a redwood tree, earth, and stone, fire, and water.

To enjoy greater Sound Health and Sound Wealth, we may wish to think of our physical selves as vessels into which we may pour Sound and Light. To improve and enjoy Sound Health, we literally enhance our vibrational patterns on a cellular level, becoming more receptive to being more <u>light</u>hearted and experiencing more en<u>light</u>enment. Although it is a lifelong process, we can *Make a Decision* to embrace new possibilities, one thought, one feeling, one breath, and one action at a time.

Human beings want and need healthy self-esteem. We want to lead good lives, and enjoy fulfillment as we do it. It's often said that our society is too materialistic and that we've become a nation of consumers, but I believe, and it is my experience, that the majority of people also have a higher degree of awareness. Most people, if you ask them to really take a moment and focus, will say that their deepest goals involve the love of their families and friends, and the wish to leave the world better than they found it, to make their own unique contribution, even if only in a small way.

The positive Spiritual aspirations that people hold in their hearts have a very fundamental relationship to their attitudes about the possibilities of well-being, material success, and prosperity. Because even if we are not consciously aware of it, we may believe that having wealth is contrary to our deepest goals. We make a distinction between money, goodness, and basic morality. From the perspective of Sound Health,

Sound Health, Sound Wealth

Sound Wealth, money is merely another form of energy, or Life Force. Many people don't think of money in Spiritual terms. Love, wisdom, inspiration, and other abstract qualities may seem to be expressions of the Divine, but money often represents a very different kind of energy. Bank accounts, car payments, and mortgages often strike us as far removed from the profound meanings of life and the Universe. We sometimes believe that Spiritual qualities cannot be touched, seen, or held in our hands. Spirituality is an internal experience. It's a feeling in our hearts and in our souls. It can't be quantified. It can't be expressed as financial wealth. This perceived opposition between Spirituality and financial wealth is more than just an oversimplification. It's the first obstacle that can be eliminated for gaining more Sound Health and Sound Wealth.

Most obstacles of this nature are based upon mistaken perceptions. Most people are comfortable with a desire for Spiritual experiences to enter their lives. It seems like a worthy aspiration. But our desire for wealth or material success can appear very different, and it can be burdened with guilt. Partly as a result of this, even if we gain wealth, we are not really fulfilled. And since at some level we might remain unhappy, our prosperity can hardly be called Sound Wealth.

If we examine the distinctions of Spirituality and wealth more closely, we know that money can come from many sources, but very often it is not seen as a manifestation of Spirit, energy, and Life Force. We might believe that money comes from clients, patients, customers, banks, or investments. It's the product of our business dealings. We may negotiate with a client, patient, or customer, for example, and if we make the appropriate transaction, the source of the money is the result of that interaction. But at a more basic level, all prosperity, including financial success, has its source in Spirit. More specifically, the special kind of prosperity that I call "Sound Wealth" comprises two elements: first, a desire for connection with the Spiritual source; and second, a desire to enjoy and share the fruits of that connection. Every form of Sound Wealth encompasses a *Divine Flow* of both giving and receiving. Receiving in itself is not enough and can leave one feeling isolated, with shame and even guilt, subconsciously or consciously.

Examples of this abound in everyday life. Love is a wonderful and empowering experience, for instance, but receiving love is only half of the equation. If we are not also giving love, we're missing perhaps the most Divine aspect of the experience itself. The very same principle applies to money. Receiving wealth is not an end in itself. It's only part of the process. Being able to make a difference in the world — by receiving and sharing — we are then able to experience the Divine aspect of Sound Health and Sound Wealth. Some people make millions of dollars, and others make billions. But if making money for oneself is the only end, <u>without exception</u>, this leads to sadness and disappointment regardless of the amount of money involved.

Sound Health, Sound Wealth

We are always deserving when we can receive rich abundance as well as share and contribute in whatever ways are appropriate for the individual, that is, <u>you</u>. When we don't enjoy the experience of wealth that includes both receiving and sharing, there are usually inner blockages of that flow emotionally, Spiritually, and even biologically. When we are accumulating not only for ourselves, we are truly free. Then the more prosperous we are, the more prosperous the world will be.

To see this rule in action, consult the biography of Andrew Carnegie, who began life as a hard-working, impoverished immigrant from Scotland and then went on to lead the United States Steel Company. Andrew Carnegie lived in the late 19th century, a time when the American economy was dominated by a small group of extremely wealthy individuals, many of whom did not live joyful and fulfilled lives. They only had lots of money. On the other hand, although Andrew Carnegie was definitely one of the wealthiest men of his time, he used the majority of his fortune to build libraries and other cultural institutions all across America so that everyone might have access to reading and cultural materials in order to learn, grow, and fulfill his or her dreams, desires, and careers. He shared his fortune in ways that felt correct for him, and in that process, assisted millions of individuals over time.

Andrew Carnegie is but one example of the many men and women who have shared their fortunes so that others could create and develop careers and personal fortunes. Oprah Winfrey and Mark Victor Hansen, author of the *Chicken Soup for the Soul* series, are contemporary examples of enlightened millionaires, especially in regard to having deep compassion for others and effecting social change, as well as sharing Life Force in the form of money.

There is an ever-growing "Natural Capitalism" that is scientifically creating a new global community, encompassing economic models that include and unite global values and biodiversity, in which everyone may prosper while restoring the natural landscape of Mother Earth. An organization called the Bioneers is one example of such a model.

If Sound Wealth was simply a matter of having a huge amount of money, the lucky men and women who have cashed multimillion-dollar lottery tickets would be the most joyful people in the world. But you know that's not the case if you've read any of the newspaper articles that regularly appear about these "big winners." Most of them won't come out and say they actually regret winning, but they certainly say that being rich hasn't turned out exactly the way they had imagined.

Chapter Eight of this book is dedicated in its entirety to defining *Sound Wealth* as "True Wealth," outlining the beliefs and blockages that can impede *Divine Flow* of Life Force in the form of money.

Sound Health, Sound Wealth

THE DECISION FOR SOUND HEALTH

Before you read any further, you may wish to play the CD enclosed in the back cover of this book. I suggest this because, as we begin to discuss topics of wellness — emotional, physical, and Spiritual — as well as rich abundance in all its pleasing forms, I want you to enjoy not only the printed page but the *Resonance* of the CD. In it are imbedded supportive messages through frequencies with sacred geometrical timing, sounds of nature, and soft intentional notes in the music itself. Please refer to the CD whenever you intuitively feel a desire to listen as you read the chapters that follow. You may play it softly in the background and let the *Resonance* of frequencies and messages soothe, support, treat, and rejuvenate you. It will also "tune" the area of your immediate environment, Body, Mind, and Spirit. The CD is soothing and relaxing but may interfere with the focus you need for precision driving or operating machinery. Therefore, you may wish to wait and listen when you are at work, home, or whenever you want to feel better with less effort.

I want to use every possible tool for communicating to you everything I've been able to learn over the course of my lifetime. With respect to health and healing, we live in a world of paradox and contradiction. On one hand, there has been enormous progress in reducing disease, alleviating pain, and extending human life. For centuries, the average life span in

Europe — and later in America — was less than 45 years, largely owing to the huge percentage of human beings who died in infancy or early childhood. Today the average life span in the developed countries is approaching 80 years — and two-thirds of all the people who <u>ever</u> reached the age of 65 are alive right now. We want to live longer, feel better, and enjoy the process. Our very success in doing so is dependent upon the small and large decisions we make in each moment and in every area of our lives.

There are as many individual perspectives on health and healing — physically, emotionally, Spiritually, and even financially — as there are individual human beings in the world. Have you ever thought about what your own perspective really is? One of my primary intentions for *Sound Health, Sound Wealth* is that by the end of the book your beliefs will be greatly clarified, if they are not already. If they are, I do hope you will find some sparkling gems to add to your "collection of ideas." This book is simply my experience, strength, and hope. It is an amalgamation of what I am still learning from both the Ancients as well as the contemporary scientific and Spiritual thinkers. It is my hope that in this process, you will feel more empowered and in control of your own health and well-being at a very core level.

What are yours ideas, beliefs, and hopes? How are they serving you? As you know, when you desire to make changes in any area of your life, it is helpful to know what you are changing <u>from</u>. To help identify your beliefs about health, healing, and abundance as they presently exist, try reading over the statements below. Do you agree with them, or disagree? Do they seem true or false? You may even want to note your responses in the margin of the page. When you look back at them after finishing the book, you may be surprised by the changes you see!

- Illness is a basic and unavoidable part of life.

- The relationship between human beings and disease is like that between a nation and an invading army.

- Illness and health are primarily manifestations of material circumstances, rather than expressions of consciousness.

- Each of us exists as a separate physical entity, and there is no way the health of one human being can benefit the health and well-being of another, much less benefit the world as a whole.

- If your genetic makeup dictates that you will get a certain illness at a specific point in your life, there is not much you can do to prevent this.

- The brain is the site of your consciousness.

- Recovery from illness means returning to the condition you were in before you became ill.

- Your economic and social origins determine your place in the world.

- If you have all your wants and needs met, without greed, others will not be able to have their needs and wants satisfied.

- If every child, woman, and man — all beings on Earth — have all their needs and wants met, without greed, you will not be able to have all your wants and needs met.

- Receiving and sharing are mutually exclusive. Wealth and riches in all areas of your life are primarily manifestations of material circumstances, rather than expressions of consciousness.

- There is no way the abundance of health and wealth of one human being can benefit the abundance of another, much less benefit the whole world.

- If you grow up in the projects and become a gang member, or you grow up in untoward circumstances, you are doomed for life.

- If you grow up in privileged circumstances, you "have it made."

- There is a finite and fixed amount of resources in the world.

- The Body, Mind, and Spirit have little or no effect on one another.

- People are intrinsically good at their core.

I will be offering my thoughts and feelings on these points throughout this book, but right now, my goal is something much more direct, and even intimate. I want to share my experience, strength, and hope with you. I am committed to inspiriting in you the "feeling belief" that wherever you are, whatever you are doing, whether you are struggling financially or a billionaire, whether you are married or single, in a great job or a "get by" job, whether you are well or sick, strong or ill, you <u>can</u> attract that which you desire — abundance in any and all forms: health, peace, hope, Faith, love, creativity, and a deeper connection with Spirit. Specifically, if you need care for your physical self, you will discover abundant resources for that purpose.

If you need a healer of any kind, you will attract the right one or ones. The *Sound Health, Sound Wealth* process will assist you to connect with the medical, naturopathic, practical, financial, and Spiritual assistance you need and desire. My experience is that we each need assistance of all kinds, physically, emotionally, and Spiritually. For the aspects of your life that you want to change, doing something different, appropriately, will give you different results. This is true for all of us, in all ways. I invite you to keep it simple and begin in this present moment. Ultimately, this is what we have: this present moment.

Making a Decision will be your most important step of all, for it creates the foundation upon which your Sound Health and Sound Wealth is built. From the moment you take this step, be prepared for exciting new synchronistic experiences. This is the radiant crystalline matrix from which you resonate frequency signals of *Your Heart's Most Treasured Desires.*

All positive outcomes are available to you by first *Making a Decision.* You do not have to know how you will achieve your outcomes, just what *Your Heart's Most Treasured Desires* are, or at least some of them. Using the concepts in *Sound Health, Sound Wealth* that resonate with you, you can and will attract the people, places, information, and synchronicities that will assist you, by being in alignment with certain Universal Principles. You will attract assistance from sources known and unknown, seen and unseen. Of course, you know that I didn't make up these principles. I have just consolidated them for you, as I have, over the years, for myself. I still use them every day and in every way, but, of course, not perfectly. You will find the Universal Principles woven throughout this book. You will also discover that for every Universal Principle, I provide simple "feeling-based" action-oriented techniques to assist you on your unique magical journey.

1) The Principle of *Resonance*: In a concert hall, were you to glide a bow across a viola, for example, all other violas in the auditorium would begin to vibrate, as they are in *Resonance*. We create a *Resonance* in the morphogenetic fields to "like" vibration when we receive back that which we give. If we want love, we give love. If we want empathy and compassion, we give empathy and compassion. If we want money, we give money. If we want the deepest magical relationships with others, we first create that deep magical relationship with our innermost selves. You can read more about this principle in Chapter One.

2) The Principle of *Future Memories*: Modern science shows that time is really nothing like the rigid commodity reported to us by clocks and watches. Actually,

time is as fluid and changeable as consciousness itself. Your consciousness can literally put you in control of time. This can fundamentally alter your life — first by giving you more time to accomplish and enjoy whatever you wish to achieve, and, in a larger sense, by altering your understanding of what life really means in an infinite context. You can read more about this principle in Chapter Two.

3) <u>The Principle of Spiritual Alchemy</u>: When we think of Alchemy, we may think of dark forces, mystical magic of turning ashes to a rose, lead to gold. Each and every atom is differentiated by its specific "song," or vibration. On the Periodic Table of Elements, the difference between lead (element #82) and gold (element #79) lies in the subtraction of three protons from the nucleus of the lead atom. The process of such transmutation requires a change in the vibrational oscillation of light, thus lead into gold. Our bodies are literally Alchemical laboratories performing trillions of vibrational Sound and Light transmutations — from one form to another on a subatomic and atomic level, in our cellular biology. Our feeling-based thoughts vibrate out into the morphogenetic fields, creating actual manifestations of our focused intent — whether for our health and well-being, or for the transformation of our relationships, our environment, and our world as a whole. You can read more about this principle in Chapter Two.

As the great physicist/philosopher Albert Einstein said: *"Imagination is more important than knowledge."* What we can imagine, with focused intent, we can create!

4) <u>The Principle of Your Magical Divine Experiment</u>™: Your *Magical Divine Experiment* is your personal unique individual experience in which you power *Your Heart's Most Treasured Desires* into actual fruition — Body, Mind, and Spirit. In your *Magical Divine Experiment* you bring your subconscious feeling-based thoughts, hopes, dreams, desires, fears, doubts, and barriers to success into full conscious awareness, in order to create the plenitude you so richly deserve. Using your expanded knowledge of your dreams, desires, strengths, and vulnerabilities, you orchestrate your thoughts, feelings, and actions so that they may become the physical, emotional, and Spiritual realities you truly desire for yourself, your loved ones, your community, the world. You can read more about this principle in Chapter Three.

5) <u>The Principle of Energetic Boundaries</u>: You can become the *Resonance* of whatever you wish to achieve. The boundaries are set by no one other than yourself. If you feel limited in any way — in Body, Mind, or Spirit — you will feel significantly empowered, not alone, as you encompass the Universe of possibilities that await you. And you <u>can</u> embrace that Universe, beginning now. You can read more about this principle in Chapter Four.

6) <u>The Positive Principle of "No"</u>: Being a positive, proactive person doesn't mean just accepting every-thing that happens, especially in a world that's perme-ated by fear and negativity in many ways. Saying "No" to toxic influences in any form — whether it's in your food and water, in the environment of your work-place, in the people who are around you in your life, or even in your innermost self — is a key step toward Sound Health and Sound Wealth — and it's a step you may never have realized you had the power to take. You can read more about this principle in Chapter Four.

7) <u>The Principle of Transforming Time</u>: The Ancients informed us and Quantum Science proved to us that time is relative. Ancients have taught us that when we are bounded by conventional time, we are spending our lives either in the future or in the past. Yet, it is from the present that we are actually creating the next experience, and then the next. Only the pres-ent moment exists, and when we focus on the present, we are miracle ready. Time, in fact, is a human con-struct that we have created for our own convenience. When we become exquisitely aware that it is our own perceptions and beliefs about time that create time itself as we experience it, we can then consciously, with specific intention, transform time. With this expanded awareness, we can expand and contract time in order to create the specific positive outcomes we desire: instant healing and munificence for ourselves, our loved ones, our community, our world. You can read more about this principle in Chapter Five.

8) <u>The Biological Principle of Hope:</u> Our bodies originate from a subatomic, unmanifest Sea of Intelligence composed of energy and information in the form of Sound and Light. We then resonate in corresponding frequencies of energy in order to manifest in the physical dimension. In other words, our unique essence originates from the macrocosm to the microcosm. As we resonate with Divine Intelligence, we appear in material form. As you resonate with hope and certainty, your material form — and the material world in which you live — is amplified in absolute congruence with *Your Heart's Most Treasured Desires.* You can read more about this principle in Chapters Six and Seven.

9) <u>The Principle of True Wealth</u>: Your inner knowing that you are creating all *Your Heart's Most Treasured Desires* actually results in the outward manifestation of all that you need and want, in ways that will absolutely astound you. The macrocosm — the external world — will actually manifest *Your Heart's Most Treasured Desires,* mirroring the microcosm, your inner world, when you practice the Principle of True Wealth. You can read more about this principle in Chapter Eight.

10) <u>The Principle of Self-Care:</u> Feeling-based Faith has the power to nurture your physical self as well as your mind and heart. Self-care is much more than just preventing or warding off illness. It is ensuring that you are and will remain the person you came into the world to be, are your highest and best, feel the most fulfilled possible in all areas of your life — blessed

with Sound Health and Sound Wealth in each moment and everything that you do and all that you are. The Principle of Self-Care is woven throughout every chapter of this book; it is one of the foundational principles of the entire book.

MANIFESTING WHAT YOU NEED AND DESIRE

I would like to close this Introduction — and begin the rest of this book — with a very moving example of the ways in which *Making a Decision* can powerfully affect your life.

Stephen was 43, happily married to his high school sweetheart, with a nine-year-old son and a daughter of seven. He had just been promoted to partner in an extraordinarily successful insurance agency. The week after his one-hundred-guest celebratory party, Stephen went to his yearly physical exam. His doctor discovered a suspicious discoloration on Stephen's back and ordered a biopsy. The biopsy diagnosed malignant melanoma. Further tests revealed that the malignant melanoma had metastasized to Stephen's liver and other major organs. He was referred to an oncologist, who told him that the cancer was so aggressive and had progressed so far that surgery, radiation, chemotherapy, and all other medical interventions would be useless. Stephen consulted three additional oncologists, who confirmed the initial diagnosis and prognosis. The physicians said all they could offer were palliative treatments of morphine for the pain that would come as the disease progressed. They advised Stephen to get his affairs in order.

Stephen's affairs were already in perfect order. He had a living will, a trust, and plenty of life insurance. He provided the same high-quality services for himself and his family that he offered to all his clients. His work was one of his passions.

Stephen and his wife Suzanne were devastated. When he looked back, Stephen realized that he hadn't actually felt ill, but in retrospect, he knew that he had felt more tired than usual for the previous six months. He had attributed his lack of energy to his recent career path.

The first couple of weeks following his devastating diagnosis, Stephen moved through shock into sadness, fear, anxiety, and grief. He could not bear the thought of leaving his wife and children. He was particularly shocked by his diagnosis and prognosis because he took such good care of himself. He exercised regularly, ate mostly organic food, and consistently made time for his family and having fun. His lifestyle was truly well balanced: Body, Mind, and Spirit.

One of Stephen's clients had a friend, Christine, who had received the same "Put your affairs in order" diagnosis from her own team of medical experts. Stephen called Christine and he and his wife agreed to meet with her at an outdoor café. Stephen couldn't hold back the tears as he looked at the sunny, clear skies that seemed to stretch forever and savored the vibrant lavenders, reds, and pinks of the flowers surrounding the patio, noticing that each flower was slightly different from the one next to it. His heart broke as he looked across at Suzanne, realizing that their dreams had turned into a nightmare.

Sound Health, Sound Wealth

Christine reached across the table and took Stephen's hands in her own. "I'm going to get right to the point here. I know from Suzanne that time is of the essence. My belief is that sometimes a life-threatening situation might be predestined in some way — that maybe it is just your time to go. Other times, I believe that if you Make a Decision *to do everything in your power to heal, you can and do heal. Everyone has his or her own path to healing, and it's different for each one of us." She handed an elegantly designed CD program to Stephen. "This is for you," she said. "It's a powerful Sound Frequency Treatment™ program. A dear friend gave it to me, and I have felt more calm, peaceful, centered, and balanced, from the very first time I listened to it. I use it at least once a day. I hope it will be as helpful to you as it has been for me."*

Christine continued, "I had a very similar experience to yours. After the shock and terror wore off, I remembered that I had actually seen some miracles myself and had heard and read about lots of other miracles. I also knew there was a scientific and Spiritual explanation for how miracles occur. I Made a Decision *to do everything in my power to create my own miracle. Thank God, I was surrounded by people who really loved me; they supported my decisions. Even if they hadn't, I would have gone forward. I knew my own truth.*

"Interestingly enough, after I Made My Decision *that miracles can and do happen, and that I was going to be one of them, a series of curious things happened. Because I felt so desperate in the beginning of this process, I was open to a lot of information that I just would have disregarded in the past.*

I was thoughtful, not impulsive, but I was profoundly aware of the clues that the Universe was sending my way.

"I could give you a hundred examples of synchronicities that have occurred in my life since I decided to create a miracle, but I'm going to describe just a little of my experience. About six months ago, I got a flyer from my local bookstore about a talk being given by a Vedic mystic. I had to ask the owner of the bookstore what Vedic *meant. I went to the talk — what's to lose, right? I learned that Vedic science contains the wisdom of five thousand years of study about the human condition — health, wellness, illness, aging — the whole schmeer. Vedic science believes that there are two signs of enlightenment: freedom from worry, and experiencing synchronicities — our recognition of magical, meaningful coincidences. Well, I am always interested in worrying less, and I was certainly ready for as many synchronistic experiences as I could have. I prayed to be open and receptive to any and all information that could help me save my own life. This Vedic talk gave me some more specific areas to investigate — more importantly, the idea that the mind is the most powerful tool we have to influence our bodies. I have learned to meditate in my own way, mainly relaxing and seeing every cell in my body as perfectly healthy, vital, and vibrating with positive energy and life. I actually had to go to the library to see photographs of healthy cells, and they are gorgeous.*

"Enlightening people, places, and opportunities to learn and experience peace and joy show up in my life, more and more frequently. I continue to listen to my heart and follow the trail of synchronistic events that magically appear."

Sound Health, Sound Wealth

Then Christine took Stephen's and Suzanne's hands, looking Stephen right in the eye. "My cancer is completely gone, or as the doctors often like to say, 'You appear to be in remission.' I know that you have your own mystical path to healing, and I believe that your path will unfold in ways that are just right for you. I am right here for both of you, to help in any way that I can. What I have been given is the great gift of living each moment as though it were my last, truly knowing that We Are All One, *and that life is just about love and compassion."*

Stephen listened to the Sound Frequency Treatment™ program several times each day. He Made a Decision *that he was willing to go to any lengths to heal himself, and he realized that real change is accomplished by taking small steps. For the first time in months, he was able to relax and sleep deeply, feeling rested in the morning. He felt inspired by the hope molecules of beta endorphins — hope powered by right action — because he believed in miracles and had an action plan to create his own.*

I spoke with Stephen a couple of weeks ago. He was five years past his diagnosis, cancer free, and "in remission." He said that his life continues to be both mysterious and magical in many ways. He continues to nurture his faith, take good care of himself, and "follow the clues" — the synchronicities that guide him toward great decisions that are just right for him. He believes without question that the mind is the most potent tool we have in relation to our bodies. He said he feels the presence of a band of angels who seem to guide his every decision.

As you apply the ideas in this book, you will certainly begin to manifest entirely new levels of health and abundance. I would love to continue to support you in this manifestation process for many years to come.

This is why I chose to create my website, www.soundhealthsoundwealth.com.

This website provides:

• A free e-newsletter with a personal message from myself each month, as well as my latest principles, strategies and tips for ongoing health and wealth.

• A "frequency treatment" room designed to accelerate the manifestation of *"Your Magical Divine Experiment*™*."*

• A Q&A section, where I answer your most important questions on how to apply the information in this book.

• Several other products and services, including my new lyrical CD *Seachange*.

Visit www.soundhealthsoundwealth.com today and sign up for my free e-newsletter!

Warmest regards,
Luanne

Sound Health, Sound Wealth

Glossary of Terms

AKASHIC RECORDS - The term coined by the Ancients for the records of all events from the beginning of time, including past, present, and future. Events may in fact be occurring at the same time in different dimensions. Quantum Physics has revealed that time itself is a construct invented by human consciousness for the purpose of creating stability, consistency, and standard ways of communicating about reality.

CRYSTALLINE LANGUAGE™ - The vibratory essence of our feeling-based thoughts and words. The more pure and positive our feeling-based thoughts and words, the more powerfully they impact the Divine Intelligence of the Quantum Hologram, creating and reflecting back to us the reality of our daily life-experience Universe. Our conscious use of Crystalline Language powerfully creates the mental, emotional, Spiritual, and physical equivalent that constructs our physical reality. In other words, every thought, intention, behavior, and action creates our life experience.

DIVINE ACTION PLAN - The planned and synchronistic "how," small step by small step, that magnetizes our dreams and pulls them into actual physical reality, now.

DIVINE TEMPLATE - Our specific goals, aspirations, hopes, and dreams, written in delicious detail, encompassing all our wants and needs: personal, interpersonal, and Altruistic — Body, Mind, and Spirit.

FUTURE MEMORY - A Future Memory may be thought of as a "vibratory blueprint," "master plan," "golden key," or "mental equivalent" from which our individual Heart's Desires may become manifest into physical form. "Future Memories" are the most effortless, concise, elegant, and individually unique "codes of creation" that interact with the Divine Intelligence of the Quantum Hologram. They are reflected back to us through synchronistic clues of the actions we need to take in order to manifest our Heart's Most Treasured Desires. Whatever our goals, aspirations, or dreams, physically, emotionally, Spiritually, and financially, we imagine these as if already accomplished now. For example, a master craftsman imagines and then creates the actual blueprint of a timeless bridge, temple, or physical structure that is well planned in exact detail. We then leave the details of how our dreams will be accomplished to Divine Intelligence, knowing that all is well.

MANIFESTATION - Creating the materialization in the physical, mental, emotional, or Spiritual world of that which did not exist before in that particular form.

QUANTUM HOLOGRAM - "The Realm of the Miraculous:" The place where energy and information combine with intention and, through Sound and

Light vibration, create actual physical matter. Each and every one of us, every unique being, person, place, and thing in the Universe is created through this process. Other names for the Quantum Hologram include the Universal Holographic Field, the Quantum Holographic Field, the Universal Hologram, and the Universal Field.

REALM OF THE MIRACULOUS - A more Spirit-based term for the Quantum Hologram. When Divine Intelligence combines science and Spirit to create all matter, producing everything that constitutes all reality.

RESONANCE - A quality of the outcome of sympathetic scientific vibrations creating perfect Oneness with the Source of All Creation. Resonance is accessed through the Quantum Hologram.

SPIRITUAL ALCHEMY - The transmutation of that which is negative into that which is positive for one and for all, through Spiritual "nonphysical, noncorporeal" means.

SYNCHRONICITY - Apparently unrelated events that co-occur in time, which are actually meaningful coincidences containing within them significant information for our particular life and our unique journey. Synchronicities provide relevant clues that are essential for fulfillment of our particular destiny.

TRUE WEALTH AND ABUNDANCE - All the ingredients we manifest now that make us whole and complete.

Sound Health, Sound Wealth

UNITY CONSCIOUSNESS - The belief that *We Are All One*. No matter how different others may appear in belief, attitude, appearance, or values, we are all profoundly more alike than we are different. The notion that diversity is necessarily bad may be an illusion, sometimes perpetuated in the service of power and control.

Chapter One

The *Principle* of *Resonance*

In order to create the profound and positive changes we wish for ourselves and our world, we need to understand and master the <u>Principle of *Resonance*</u>: perfect oneness with the Source of All Creation. *Resonance* is accessed through our connection with the *Quantum Hologram*, which I personally also think of as *The Realm of the Miraculous*, the place where energy and information combine with intention to vibrate into matter, actually creating each and every unique being on this planet.

The experience of *Resonance* is marked by a chemical phenomenon in which the valence electrons of a molecule change back and forth between two or more states. Scientifically, *Resonance* is characterized by a larger than normal frequency vibration. *Resonance* is an interactive frequency, a magnetic energetic attraction that draws us to a person, a place, meaningful experiences, a career, certain tastes, and particular music. If we listen carefully to the center and core of our very being, *Resonance* reveals clues that point the way to our life purpose, our destiny, and *Our Heart's Most Treasured Desires*. True *Resonance* is the heart and soul of all that calls to us. To be our highest and best, we must respond with our whole beings.

Sound Health, Sound Wealth

My own earliest memories of *Resonance* were my special connections with old people, animals, babies and children, the ocean, and music. I began piano lessons at five, and I remember exactly how I felt when I struck a major seventh chord. I felt the ocean! Years later, I came to believe that ocean waves actually come in on a major seventh chord, and go out on a minor one. The *Resonance* of music and the ocean connects in me in a profound way that I understood intellectually only much later in my life. I heard and felt the way Sound resonated in the bodies of people and animals, and that *Resonance* told me what to seek out and what to avoid. I was becoming a medical and Spiritual intuitive. I believe that we all are "inituitives" depending on our level of focus and experience.

Just as we all do, consciously and subconsciously, I began to sense <u>dissonance</u> and *Resonance* in various people and situations. I have always loved to sing. I picked up a guitar for the first time when I was 10 ... I fell immediately and profoundly in love. The same was true with the flute and recorder, at 17. Music was a way to express my thoughts and feelings in a positive form. I have known for a long time that music has been one of the most important keys to my emotional balance. Through my music, I could clear out the storms, connect with Divine Source and the deepest part of myself, create something unique, and connect with others.

Throughout this chapter, and indeed, throughout this entire book, you will find examples that illustrate the ways we use *Resonance* as our magical, scientific Divine springboard to Sound Health, Sound Wealth. But enjoying Sound Health and Sound Wealth is not an abstract concept. What tangible benefits would you like to gain from this experience? What are *Your Heart's Most Treasured Desires* for yourself, for those you love, and for the world?

Here, at this place in your own particular journey into genuine health and wealth, it is important to answer these questions as clearly as possible. To help you in this clarification process, look at the examples below. What elements in each vignette resonate to you?

Robin is a married woman with three children. She works part time out of her home as a designer of children's clothing. Robin just celebrated her 40th birthday, and this milestone has made her aware of some changes that have taken place in her physical self. Although she doesn't feel sick, she knows she doesn't have the energy she used to have. She sometimes takes naps in the afternoon before the kids come home from school. This is something she would never have done even five years earlier. What's more, she recently became aware of occasional numbness in her hands and feet, especially when she wakes up from a nap. This, too, is an experience she had never had in the past, and she has found it rather frightening. As a result, she had a complete physical examination — which, as it turned out, indicated she was in perfect health. But her family doctor's reassurances did not completely satisfy Robin. She remains frightened that something is wrong with her. She keeps these fears to herself, how-

ever, especially since, in her last call to her doctor, he seemed to suggest that she might be depressed and could benefit from an antidepressant medication. Robin experiences anxiety about how her health and functioning could impact her husband, her three children, and their financial well-being. Robin contributes more than half of the family income.

Paul is a 53-year-old attorney who recently underwent an angioplasty procedure to alleviate a potentially dangerous cardiovascular condition. Unlike Robin, Paul knows all too well what his problem is and where it is located. He is now following a carefully regulated program of diet, exercise, and medication. Paul has a great deal of trust in his doctors and in the powers of Western medicine, but he has also done some reading about the benefits of holistic approaches and the Spiritual aspects of illness and health. Paul is not sure exactly how much he believes of what he's read, but he wants to learn more about the relationship of Body, Mind, and Spirit He wants to explore both the philosophical and practical elements of non-Western approaches to healing. Like Robin, Paul has significant concerns about how any change in his ability to earn could impact his wife and his elderly mother, who lives with them.

Jane is a full-time college student and a part-time athlete. She is an experienced runner and rock climber. At this point,

she has no health concerns whatsoever, at least for herself. She is very concerned, however, about her grandmother, who is undergoing cancer treatment. Jane is interested in learning about how one person can benefit the healing processes of another, whether through prayer, meditation, or simply sharing Spiritually oriented ideas and teachings. More specifically, Jane wants to learn whether there is anything else she can do to help her beloved grandmother get well, even if this requires somehow bringing a "miracle" into the world. She wants to believe that this is possible, and she wants to find information that can reinforce this belief.

These examples represent three perspectives on issues of health and abundance. They are different beliefs about <u>what is possible.</u> There are people who have a health concern that conventional medicine has not been able to treat, or even to identify, and they are looking for holistic viewpoints. Others have a problem that has been diagnosed all too clearly, and they wish to explore every possible avenue of treatment, in addition to those offered by mainstream medicine. Still others have no immediate concern for themselves, but they want to know what they can do for others. In the fabric of these stories, and woven throughout our lives as well, are our conscious and subconscious beliefs about abundance in all forms — health, relationships, peace, contentment, and wealth. How much can we have? Can we have what we want and need without diminishing others, or the world?

Sound Health, Sound Wealth

THE UNITY OF BODY, MIND, AND SPIRIT

When I use the words *Body, Mind, and Spirit*, there is an implied separation among these concepts and functions. Somehow, the words themselves suggest "differentness." Our very language reflects the schism that exists in our thinking — the implication that Body, Mind, and Spirit are separate domains that function separately. In truth, we are all whole and complete beings, and there is absolutely no intrinsic or real separation of Body, Mind, and Spirit. These three elements of Being are always interconnected and instantaneously interactive.

When we make a change in any area of our functioning, that change resonates with all other areas of our functioning. Making lifestyle changes, for example, to be more physically fit and strong changes our physiology immediately — our bodies and immune systems instantaneously feel better, and function better, before we ever set foot in a gym, hike a mountain trail, or walk the mall. In turn, our minds function more efficiently, our self-esteem (being competent and feeling worthy) improves, and our connection with Spirit is strengthened because we have moved into action to become more balanced. Authentic balance always resonates with Spirit. Interestingly enough, when we change, those around us change. Every change we make impacts our immediate ecosystem of relationships and experiences, and reverberates into the larger ecosystem in which *We Are All One.*

Sound Health, Sound Wealth resonates with the Universal Laws that organize the *Quantum Hologram.* The Quantum Hologram is composed of energy and information, which, when combined with intention, creates trees, oceans, rivers, mountains, cities, animals, works of art — and also you and me. Each creation of matter is unique, with its own distinctive energetic, atomic, and molecular structure. All dogs are not the same dog: Each is absolutely one of a kind. From the Parthenon, to a new rosebud you noticed this morning as you walked in to work, each and every creation is sole and special. Each of us shares common characteristics with our species and other species, but everything is one of a kind, from the Great Pyramid, to a blade of grass, to your new "most beautiful baby in the world."

I would like to share more of my own early life experiences with you. I would like you to know how I have discovered, created, used (and still use) the foundational Principle of *Resonance*. I am nearly 54 years old and have never felt better or more blissful in my life. Most of the information in this book is the result of why this is so. I do not wish this to be a treatise on "Woundology," but I do feel that, regardless of our hurts and traumas, whatever they may be, there is no scorecard for their severity. Nor do we have to experience actual traumas in order to become disheartened, dispirited, depressed, suicidal, or physically ill. Moreover, it is how, when, and what assistance we create and attract for ourselves that heals us and

Sound Health, Sound Wealth

allows us to experience the "bliss" our Body, Mind, and Spirit has in store for us as our birthright. After you read this book, you will decide whether you also believe that this is so.

In my senior year of high school, I fell from a high swing, broke my neck, and spent months of my senior year in the hospital, recuperating in traction. Before graduating from high school, I was hit by a car. My ribs and back were severely injured. From a horse-back-riding accident, I was hospitalized for contusion of the spine, a cracked patella, and a fracture of the tibia. In another accident, our car was broadsided by a drunk driver who left the scene. The car was totaled and I suffered a fractured elbow and severe whiplash.

I entered this life with scoliosis and a genetically poor immune system. There was much trauma at home, partially due to alcoholism. Throughout child-hood and into early adulthood, I had chronic tonsilli-tis and, following my tonsillectomy, strep throat. Traditional medicine worked only to a point, and I developed antibiotic resistance early in life.

I began to sing when I was very young. Looking back, I know that singing saved my life. I sang because I intuitively knew that sound vibrations helped me heal. As a child, adolescent, and young adult, I fought undiagnosed depression and anxiety, and from post-traumatic stress disorder and attention-deficit disorder with hyperactivity. Needless to say, I had a lot of physical and emotional trauma. This is why I believe that if someone like me can feel bliss the majority of the time, there is hope for anyone. In addition, there are many who suffer much worse trauma, who live whole and complete lives feeling a bliss and connectedness to all, and that astounds me still.

I wrote and played music professionally from my early teens. When I was 14 years old, I worked a whole summer without any payment for a superb veterinarian, Dr. Royal Erhardt Klofanda. Eventually, because of my persistence and willingness to learn his strict standards of treatment, he gave me a job with a salary. We developed a special relationship, both Spiritual and magical, over the years. We shared the world of ideas, a passionate interest in many modalities of natural healing, and, although I didn't know its name at the time, a mutual understanding of Quantum Physics. My summer job turned into a unique mentorship that lasted more than a decade.

In a storage area of his animal hospital, I found a worn black leather medical bag that had once belonged to Royal's father, a country veterinarian. In this ancient-looking bag were a variety of surgical tools, as well as metal tuning forks from Germany. When I learned from Royal that tuning forks had historically been used to detect bone fractures — a sound frequency technology that used *Resonance,* I began experimenting with them, to diagnose and treat our animal patients. I also learned to use the tuning forks on myself for healing bumps, scrapes, and fractures, as well as for increasing my own well-being.

Sound Health, Sound Wealth

I discovered that loving and compassionate intentions, choosing specific vibrations from selected tuning forks, and using keys and tones in my own voice, had a powerfully positive impact on the healing time of my "furry patients."

Not long after my discoveries about the healing power of *Resonance*, I was terrified when my beloved and deaf dalmatian, Mickbookanook, was hit by a car. His pelvis was horribly fractured, one hip was shattered, and he had serious internal bleeding. Royal lovingly and compassionately encouraged me to euthanize Mickbookanook, because of his very compromised prognosis. I just couldn't do it. I used my intention, prayer, tuning forks, my voice, massage, the laying on of hands, whirlpool therapy — anything and everything I could think of to save him. Incredibly, Mickbookanook survived. I wish I had kept the X-rays. His body actually created a new functional hip socket. He lived a long, rich life, running on the beach with me almost daily.

It was after Royal retired that I became a nurse, in my early twenties, supporting myself by working in the health field and performing music. Both professions were suffused with *Resonance* for me. In nursing, I practiced a variety of holistic healing modalities, including medical intuition (a conduit connected with the *Quantum Hologram*), as well as practices which are now recognized as Sound treatment technologies. In those days, all my clients were either physicians or nurses.

One
The Principle of Resonance

54

In my mid-twenties, I made the full circle back to Holistic Medicine. Remaining open-minded to "all traditions for healing and well-being" honors each unique individual who is in need of assistance. The many wondrous healing approaches may include ancient philosophies such as Ayurveda, naturopathic and vibrational medicine of all types, Spirituality, and the most useful of allopathic contemporary medical scientific breakthroughs.

I somehow knew that music and holistic science and practice would together create my path to healing. I am grateful for the celestial clues about healing, health, and wellness that appeared along my path. I am now a doctor of Holistic Science, still a singer/ songwriter/musician, and have been creating "Frequency Treatments™" (although I only began using that term in the 1970s) since my childhood and early teens.

The Principle of Resonance contains within it the Universal Laws that organize the Quantum Hologram of all that is possible. The Quantum Hologram is composed of energy and information, which, when combined with intention, creates matter: an instantaneous continuous process of sending and receiving, from the macrocosm to the microcosm and back, interacting, moving, and flowing. This process creates, sustains, and changes each of us, our world, and the Universe. Our beliefs determine our reality. Our reality affects the reality of others and of the world.

Sound Health, Sound Wealth

In my twenties, I was hit by an emergency health crisis. Thankfully, I was able to integrate these tools of *Resonance* and make life-saving use of them on my own healing journey. I had suddenly become ill and required emergency surgery. I knew that I had to move beyond conventional methods in order to manifest my *Heart's Desire* for getting well. I also knew that decisions made with my whole being could have entirely different outcomes than those made from intellect or intuition alone. Our thoughts are most powerful when they resonate with our hearts. So I decided to use the power of my mind and my heart to deal with my life-threatening challenge in the most positive way I could.

THE *RESONANCE* OF THE HEART

I realized that I had to have my intellect in authentic *Resonance* with my heart in order to make a series of critical life-changing decisions. Decisions made from the heart can have entirely different outcomes than decisions made from the mind or the body alone. Our intellect is best used when combined with the *Resonance of the Heart*. <u>The accuracy of the saying "The Heart Knows" rings through the centuries with clarity, like the chiming of ancient bells.</u> How many times have you heard the phrase "I just knew in my heart that it was the right decision," or, "My heart told me that this just wouldn't work"? Words like, *heartfelt, hearth, hearty, heart-to-heart, heartwarming, heartrending, heartbroken, heartless, heartsick, heartache, heartthrob, heart of gold, heartburn*

— these words impact us with immediacy and essential truth.

I knew in my heart that I had to focus on manifesting everything I needed through what I had learned about synchronicity, faith, *Resonance*, and Divine Source.

I knew that, if we are paying attention, synchronistic events contain rich layers and levels of meaning. When these events are correctly interpreted and understood, they provide significant information about how to move through your life to create all that you want and need. I knew in the deepest core of my being that the only way to heal myself was through my belief in Unity Consciousness — my belief that ultimately *We Are All One.* That meant I had to truly believe that all I needed would be provided to me if I used my understanding of synchronicity, the timeless Laws of Manifestation, and Unity Consciousness, with a passionate willingness to follow the clues that the Universe would provide me.

First, as I described in the Introduction to this book, I *Made a Decision* that I would completely heal in Body, Mind, and Spirit. I then put in writing exactly what I needed and wanted in order to heal. I was extremely specific, describing everything I desired in extreme detail. I copied this onto cards that I carried with me, and I read them at least three times a day. One of my desires took the form of a crystal-clear feeling-based visualization. I imagined living in a beautiful home with lots of light, near a path that led down to a beach — to make a long story short, I found just the home I had imagined and prayed for. There was only one problem: I did not have quite enough money to pay the deposit for utilities. I was short by exactly $227. It seemed like a million dollars to me at the time.

Just before sunrise while meditating on the still-wet beach, I placed my forehead on the damp sand — something I had never done before. I asked Divine Presence for assistance emotionally, physically, and Spiritually. As I raised my head toward the spectacular sunrise, I noticed something I was sure hadn't been there just a moment before — a clump of seaweed, sparkling with tiny saltwater bubbles, which had washed up on the sand right next to me. Tangled in the seaweed was wet crumpled money — $227, in twenties, tens, and ones. The exact amount I needed to make my move. I was awed, elated, and relieved.

I realized that the magical oceanic treasure that had washed up on the beach that early morning was a clear and direct *Resonance* answer to *My Heart's Most Treasured Desire*, manifested through the "meaningful coincidence" of synchronicity.

THE PROCESS OF MANIFESTATION

From these experiences I learned that writing down *My Heart's Most Treasured Desires*, specifically and in Technicolor detail, was absolutely significant in the manifestation process. It makes complete sense. I wrote them, said them aloud, felt them, and envisioned these things to utilize all parts of my Body/Mind. The Universe can deliver exactly what you want and need only if you compose your "en-mail" ("energetic mail") in exquisite detail, accompanied by your feeling-based certainty that you will be answered by Divine Source through synchronicity. Sometimes, you have to unravel the clues in order to understand the mystery code that allows you to manifest your request. In the manifestation process we, with the assistance of intention and our connection with the *Quantum Hologram*, materialize what we need and desire. There is a way in which our whole beings must be in true *Resonance* with our *Heart's Desire* in order to create the biochemistry that provides support on a cellular level for the physical manifestation of what we need.

Whatever abundance you wish, whatever you need and desire — emotionally, materially, physically, mentally, and Spiritually — is available to you. What you desire can and will have a better chance of showing up for you if you clarify your template of what you want and need and take concise actions — holding your needs in your heart and Spirit — and persevere. Never give up. Never!

CRYSTALLINE LANGUAGE™:
A GOLDEN KEY TO RESONANCE
AND TO MANIFESTING
YOUR HEART'S MOST TREASURED DESIRES

In my twenties, when I wanted to experience manifestation emotionally, physically, and Spiritually, I made bold statements like, "I will accomplish this goal or die trying." A close friend, Robert, a wealthy retired businessman, had spent considerable time in India seeking peace and enlightenment. He helped me understand more clearly that "thoughts indeed do become things." He suggested that I consider refining my language for my own benefit, and even for my own safety. Robert asked me to consider changing my brash "I will die trying" statement, and say instead, "I will live fully each day, enjoying the journey, and accomplish *My Heart's Most Treasured Desires*, benefiting myself, all others, and the world."

From Robert, I became aware of the extraordinary significance of how the specific words I chose to use directly influenced the outcomes I experienced. I discovered how to use language as a crystal messenger, understanding even more deeply that words are thoughts that really do become things.

Just as atoms form specific structures such as beautiful gems, the same is true in all manifestation processes — including the creation and perfection of the radiant cells in your body. In the same way that gems and cells are created from subatomic energy, information, and intention, the conscious use of thoughts, words, and sounds, vibrate into matter, from the invisible to the visible, affecting all outcomes in your life. In the same way, subconscious thoughts and feelings also vibrate into matter, which is why it is absolutely essential to bring the subconscious into conscious awareness.

Understanding this vibratory process of *Resonance* assists you to manifest your dreams. I came to think of this specific technique as using what I call *Crystalline Language*™. Sounds, forming words and contained in thoughts, become subatomic messengers to whatever name you wish to call the omnipresent organizing architect of our Universe. I understood that actual sounds — syntax, tone, and pitch — along with thoughts and feelings, become vibratory messengers that interact with all of life through the *Quantum Hologram.* I used this now-conscious knowledge in very practical ways, for myself and for all others. For example, when I found myself experiencing anxiety and fear about taxes, I observed that by moving these very human thoughts and feelings quickly out of my being, Body, Mind, and Spirit, I created space for positive healing and manifestation, and the money for my taxes appeared right when I needed it. I gradually transformed fear into faith, and still do today. I believe this is a lifelong process for me, and sometimes, a moment-by-moment practice.

Because we know that thoughts become things, the process of refining our thoughts and feelings into crystalline purity, using *Crystalline Language*, helps them become the things that we really desire — impacting our relationships with ourselves, all others, and the world in which we live.

Like our thoughts, words, and feelings, our bodies are literally crystalline structures. Our bones, for example, are composed of calcium crystals that vibrate like tuning forks. The colors of our internal organs, blood, and cellular fluids are specific colors that vibrate at different frequencies. *Sound Health, Sound Wealth* illuminates the specific techniques that you will recognize as perfect for your particular vibrant *Resonance.*

WE ARE LITERALLY 'BEINGS OF SOUND AND LIGHT'

Both Sound and Light originate from photons from the Sun. These photons nourish plant life and the atmosphere, and are significant ingredients for the health and well-being of us, all living beings, Mother Earth, and the stratosphere. Sound and Light are approximately 40 octaves apart. All Light and colors originate from Sound. The well-known phrase "First, there was the Word" is a biblical reference that was proven to be scientifically accurate decades ago. All colors have a specific measurable vibrational frequency. For example, shades and hues of red vibrate to the key of C. I have learned that Sound and Light, when used with precision and specific intention, can heal and balance organs, blood, cells, and all metabolic processes. Sound and Light are used with increasing frequency as they are rediscovered by Western medicine for diagnosis and treatment. Sound and Light have been utilized by ancient cultures on all seven continents across the millennia for healing humans and animals, creating a symbiotic nurturing relationship with Nature, as well.

MAKING YOUR DREAMS A REALITY

Sound Health, Sound Wealth is different for each of us, depending on our particular circumstances. As we are exposed to the Technology of *Resonance,* we choose the specific tools and techniques that reverberate distinctively for us, at a unique time in our lives. As we change and develop, our selection from the symphony of *Resonance* may change over time, or even within a single day.

Victor was a nurse who had tripped over a cement parking curb at a hamburger stand and hit his head, resulting in a brain injury that caused him to be a quadriplegic. Victor had the misfortune of being immobilized, but with severe pain. He was 40 years old. I was the charge nurse for Victor in an overcrowded, understaffed, underbudgeted rehabilitilitation/convalescent hospital. Victor lived in reverence for each sip of water or bite of food. He nurtured and oversaw the needs and the care of four other patients in his room, whom he considered less fortunate than himself. These four patients were in desperate despair, with debilitating injuries, major mental disorders, and very poor prognoses. Victor con-

sidered his internal Universe beautiful and majestic. He told me that he often left his body and traveled the world in his meditations, prayers, and dreams.

Victor was an important mentor to me, showing me what is possible in what I considered his horrific circumstance. One time he had a nurses' aide pick an exquisitely fragrant cream and crimson rose and put it in a Dixie cup for me. He also gave me a United States silver half-dollar, dated 1945, the year of his birth. He pointed out that by subtracting the date of my birth from the date of his birth left the number eight — the symbol of Infinity. He smiled and said I might search for the meanings of his gift over time. I wondered where he had gotten it. I knew he was penniless. One side of the coin depicted an eagle, wings powerfully raised, with the phrase "E PLURIBUS UNUM." On the other side of the half-dollar were Lady Liberty, welcoming arm outstretched, flowing robes, and the phrase "IN GOD WE TRUST." "E PLURIBUS UNUM" was the motto proposed for the first Great Seal of The United States by John Adams, Benjamin Franklin, and Thomas Jefferson in 1776. A Latin phrase meaning "One from Many," the phrase stated the determination to form a single nation from a collection of states. Over subsequent years, "E PLURIBUS UNUM" signified America's attempt to create one unified nation of people from many different backgrounds and beliefs, seeking unity while respecting diversity. Current United States silver half-dollars depict a rampant bald eagle, grasping an olive branch as an offering of peace; the eagle also holds a clutch of arrows as an alternative when peace is rejected. Surrounding patterns represent peoples of the world whose contributions have forged

American culture. Behind the head of the eagle is a Native American design from a Hopi vase. Under the right wing is a representation of the special contribution of the Jews. Under the left wing is a European design from a classical Greek ceramic vessel. (This information was obtained from the E Pluribus Unum Project.)

Victor lived the principles of Sound Health, Sound Wealth, every moment of every day that I was privileged to know him. He is a shining beacon of faith for me. Without him, this book would not have the depth and breadth I strive for.

CREATING RESONANCE

I would not be writing a book if I did not believe that writing creates a special connection with the Inner Spirit, as well as with the energies that infuse the Universe as a whole. For this reason, I am going to ask you to consider making a commitment to create this connection for yourself. Simply put, I am going to consider asking you to write a bit. Please follow the steps below to get this process started by acquiring and beginning a personal journal. Throughout this book, we'll use your journal as a tool for quickly summing up and connecting with the substance of what we've discussed.

1. To begin, you can obtain a beautiful or handsome journal or notebook and a pen or pencil that you really like from your favorite gift shop. These can be tools for your Alchemical transformation.

2. Make a detailed assessment of exactly where you are in your life right now. Assess your intimate relationships, friendships, work, play, Spirituality, physical exercise, nutrition, health, relaxation and fun, your home, the quality of your time alone, hobbies, interests, and use of alcohol, drugs, cigarettes, cigars, and pipes, as well as your use of prescription and over-the-counter drugs. Be excruciatingly honest — down to your very core. Keep it simple. This is for your eyes only. Do your assessment with objectivity, compassion, and <u>without judgment</u> — just as you would do an objective assessment of a loved one or dear friend, in order to assist that person. Use your best intellectual and intuitive skills — the same skills that you call on to choose a new vehicle, consider a job change, select day care for your precious child, or make a significant health decision about your family or loved ones. Consider reversing the Golden Rule with compassion: "Do unto yourself as you would do unto others."

Put a plus in the areas of your life that are working well for you, and a minus in the areas that are not working the way you would like. In the areas that are difficult or painful, ask for Divine Assistance and Guidance, or, in your own unique way, connect with your "Truth Center." Make an intuitive list of the blocks, or problems, that seem to impede your progress, the things that seem to make it impossible for you to achieve what you desire.

This process will bring the subconscious blocks into your conscious awareness, if you so desire. For example, a blockage might be, "I never have time to work on my creative projects, to exercise, or have fun." Creating an empowering statement to your Subconscious Mind might read like this:

One
The *Principle* of
Resonance

66

"I, _____, NOW arrange my life in ways that assist me to rest, rejuvenate, create, dream, and imagine. I give myself the time and space that I need. I am infused with more energy, pleasure, and life satisfaction. I have an increasing amount of faith, ease, joy, and peace in my life Now! My enhanced self-care is benefiting all those around me. I radiate peace, joy, and abundance, and it synchronistically returns to me from sources known and unknown. I am surrounded in Loving, Harmonious Relationships."

Use language that resonates for you! In this way, more will be revealed in a more effortless fashion. As A Course in Miracles® says, "Love brings up anything unlike itself."

Honest self-assessment allows you to take credit for your strengths and successes, no matter how small you might be inclined to make them. Bask in the radiant glow of the <u>small daily positive steps</u> that you take to make your life better, every day and in every way. Identify your problematic areas, and *Make a Decision* to finish this chapter, in a way that is correct for you.

3. Sit in a comfortable position in a pleasing environment. Make simple and concise notes about *Your Heart's Most Treasured Desires*, one for each area of your life, Body, Mind, and Spirit. Write down a time frame that intuitively feels right for you. Use *Crystalline Language*™. Remember, <u>your</u> "Word is your Wand." Write your Desires in the present tense.

4. Transfer *Your Heart's Most Treasured Desires* into your elegant notebook or journal.

5. Write your desired outcomes on a three-by-five-inch (or smaller) card, and laminate it (if you like this idea) so that you can carry it with you easily. If

you wish, make the desired outcomes colorful. Read your outcomes with feeling, and focus on them a minimum of three times a day, or whenever you need to interrupt a negative pattern of thought.

6. Take the time to imagine how it will feel as you experience each of *Your Heart's Most Treasured Desires* becoming manifest, regardless of how audacious they may seem. One day they will not seem so. Use all of your senses to create a rich, multidimensional, full-spectrum "feeling-based" reality.

Adopt the physiology of how you will feel when your dreams come true. Stand tall, and "hold your vessel higher to be filled." It will be. You will attract assistance in surprising ways. You are the only one who can do this for yourself. Breathe in the richness of life.

Put a "sparkle in your eyes and a smile on your face." When you are ready, move on to the next chapter.

Chapter Two

The *Principle* of *Future Memories*

Right now, what is the quality of your life? To what extent does your life feel synchronistic or magical? Do you think it is possible for you to have more time and more fun? Can you imagine adding more value to your life and to the lives of others — emotionally, physically, Spiritually, and even financially? Total abundance in these areas is not only possible, it is the ever-increasing actual outcome of your *Future Memories.*

You can have the fulfillment you seek. You can manifest *Your Heart's Most Treasured Desires*; the key is to first change your thoughts — the thought forms that link directly to the *Quantum Hologram*. As I've mentioned before, the *Quantum Hologram* is the omniscient, omnipotent presence that organizes your intentions and orchestrates the unlimited field of energy, information, and intention, from which all matter is created. I also resonate to the language of calling the *Quantum Hologram* "Divine Intelligence." You will of course use the term for this creative presence that is appropriate to you.

FUTURE MEMORIES

Extraordinary musical compositions, fine art, and ancient structures — pyramids, temples, churches, bridges, and castles — remain beautifully intact, over hundreds and thousands of years, in every part of the world. Many of these masterpieces have survived violent storms, tsunamis, earthquakes, tornadoes, and volcanic eruptions.

Before a master craftsperson can build a beautiful structure, it must first be alive as a "thought form." This structure begins as an internal vision or dream, essentially an intangible blueprint, which became manifest in physical form. The architect couldn't have experienced the vision without also having the feeling-based belief that the idea could enter the physical realm. This process is interactive. The architect continually interacts with the *Quantum Hologram*, sending and receiving intention, energy, and information. And so the process goes, from within to without, from microcosm to macrocosm. Finally, when the building itself is completed, it has an impact on all who see it, use it, and know about it. There is an ongoing energetic interaction between the creator, the creation, the world, and the *Quantum Hologram*.

Sometimes the viability of these works of art seems to defy our human understanding. How can this be? We stand in awe and wonder. The duration of these treasures over the test of time is due to the constant exquisite interaction between the architect

and the *Quantum Hologram,* in alignment with the timeless flow of the enduring Laws of Creation. These
Laws are expressions of an intuitive mathematical
grace that creates a literal and measurable "magnetic
tension." This magnetic tension is what keeps structures such as pyramids, beautiful bridges, and temples
in place. You refine your own intuitive mathematical
grace as you learn how to consciously tap into the
unseen natural laws, using them to bring to fruition
your fulfillment, each and every day.

What you've just read is more than a philosophical
viewpoint. The truth is, you are the architect and master craftsperson of your own life. At every moment,
you create and modify your own internal blueprint,
consciously and subconsciously. In this process, you
sometimes fine-tune a detail, and sometimes you do
major renovations. Your goal is always to create, small
step by small step, the results you desire in all areas of
your life.

This chapter will provide a powerful technique for
using feeling-based faith to care for your thoughts and
emotions, and for your physical well-being also. The
technique is the creation of *Future Memories* that can
transform your life in profound and wondrous ways.
Future Memories are your specific goals, hopes, dreams,
and desires, which you experience in exquisite detail
through your Body, Mind, and Spirit. You create your
Future Memories as though they have already occurred so
that your goals and dreams are already a tangible reality. A *Future Memory* sends a packet of energy contain-

ing the spectral rays of *Your Heart's Most Treasured Desires* into the *Realm of the Miraculous*. This in turn unfolds a series of wondrous and synchronistic events that draw you toward the magical and fulfilling destiny that you have already brought into being by creating your *Future Memories*.

Here's one example of how this takes place ...

I rode my bicycle to the locked gate of the mansion. I identified myself, showing my driver's license. "Straight ahead to the house. You can't miss it." A lush emerald lawn seemed to stretch forever down the long driveway that led to the entrance of the house, three imposing stories of luminous weathered granite, four graceful columns in front. It was gorgeous, impressive, with not a hint of ostentation.

My job that week through the nursing registry was to provide post-surgical care to an older patient. All I had to do was administer three intramuscular injections per day of medication, and to check George's vital signs. I was a bit concerned that the week was going to drag along. However, Helen, George's charming and gracious wife, said she was feeling pretty stiff and old and asked me some questions about her own health, and how to feel better.

I designed an exercise program for Helen that involved walking and mild Yoga stretching on the lush grounds of the couple's beautiful oceanfront estate. By the end of the week, Helen was feeling more hopeful, vibrant, and alive. We had a great time and lots of laughs. She said she would call to let me know how she was doing with her program.

George and Helen encouraged me to make myself at home and look around as much as I wanted. A hundred-foot-long ballroom contained floor-to-ceiling bookshelves, filled with books on an enormous variety of subjects. The books were so diverse and wide-ranging that I couldn't figure out what could possibly tie the whole collection together. Curious, I asked them what their particular interest was. They told me their life passion had been, and still was, writing.

As I sipped English tea, it was a great pleasure to hear the success story of this courageous elderly couple. With no particular training or experience, they set off in their old beat-up jalopy, as they referred to it, and left the security of their parents' farm in the Midwest. They packed two small children and a few possessions into the old car. They had $300 and a big dream as they set off for Hollywood in the early 1950s.

The couple's family and friends were disappointed and critical of the couple's foolhardy dream of creating a daytime television drama. George and Helen had each other, a dream they shared, and the courage to set off into a new life. They had Made a Decision, *and for them, there was no turning back. Once they landed in Hollywood, their enthusiasm and passion to live their dream was contagious. Their complete commitment — Body, Mind, and Spirit — allowed them to recognize and experience a cornucopia of magical synchronistic events. Eighteen months after they arrived in Hollywood, their pilot for a daytime television drama was the sough-after prize in a bidding war among the major networks. They kept their vision alive by creating* Future Memories, *individually and together, every day. They also practiced envisioning and feeling their dream's continuing success, in spite of the notorious unpredictability of the television business.*

George and Helen were pleased about the money that multiplied each year, but the real payoff for them was the pleasure of breathing life into the characters they had created over the years, and the evolving story. That peerless television drama is still alive and well, and on the air today.

What a pleasure and joy it was to spend that week with them. We sat on their beautiful balcony, eating lovely food served by delightful staff. George and Helen told me they were still amazed by the wealth their series had provided — that was a bountiful side effect of the continued joy that their creativity, faith, and courage had brought. The most important thing to them was that they had lived their dream and experienced deep fulfillment. Even after retirement, they continued to write for their program as consultants.

Looking back, I would have gladly paid Helen and George for the experience they so kindly shared with me. I learned exactly how they turned their dream into a reality that brought them joy and satisfaction every single day. They told me their secret to success was very simple: Faith, Perseverance, *Making a Decision*, and continually creating *Future Memories*.

KEEPING YOUR VISION ALIVE

Just as you can manifest everything you desire, you must also accept accountability if you receive something less than what you desire. When you settle for less, you receive less. If you choose to be "average," you will be average. This is true in all areas of our lives. If, for example, you accept a medical diagnosis based on statistical averages, you could very well experience compromised health, or even lose your life.

To create a statistical average for a particular diagnosis, medical researchers combine the results of the best-possible- case scenario (cured), with the results of the worst-possible- case scenario, along with all the case results that fall in between. They then add the individual results together and divide by the number of individuals being studied, producing the "average." Most health-treatment plans use this average as the foundation for treatment. This averaging process is rarely explained, and it has caused pain and, sometimes, real damage for a significant number of people.

"Average" doesn't describe any of us accurately. Each and every person is a unique expression of Divine Intelligence, differentiated and totally unique in the physical world of matter through DNA.

Many people diagnosed with grave medical conditions — often statistically given only months to live — have miraculously survived and even completely healed. In order for this healing to happen, it was essential for the individual to change his or her internal blueprint. He or she had to believe that a miracle was possible and that a miracle could and would be created for total healing.

Sound Health, Sound Wealth

Most cancer survivors have absolutely refused to accept the death sentence "We can't do anything more for you. You need to get your affairs in order." Cancer survivors refuse to base their own unique, irreplaceable, precious lives on being average. Those who "beat" cancer, or any life-threatening illness, have to make use of their thinking and feeling skills, deepen their faith, gather significant information from a variety of sources, put together the right team to support them, and act as though they are not going to accept being a statistic. They create a different process, and, often, a very different outcome.

Cultural beliefs often create roadblocks to manifestation of your real self. Cultural and subcultural beliefs often define being "different" as bad. There are sometimes severe negative sanctions for stepping outside the norm. Cultural myths would have us believe that artists must starve, that genius must suffer, and that excellence in one's personal interests and desires is reserved for the privileged few. History and current reality refute these myths. It is imperative not to acquiesce to these myths and accept less than you truly deserve. Instead, go forward and live your life at your very highest and best, in all that you do. This is your true destiny, the reason you are here in the world.

If you grew up in poverty, you may have come to believe that poverty is your inevitable destiny. If you grew up privileged, your own and others' expectations may have led you to set unrealistically high goals for yourself. This can backfire, creating significant anxiety and depression when you can't do everything perfectly. Or, you may feel that your privilege exempts you from the foundational work and tenacity required to discover and live your life's purpose. Anxiety, depression, and, perhaps, even self-absorption may cause you to fail miserably.

None of these beliefs are congruent with your intrinsic abilities to profoundly change yourself and your life in positive ways. We know that many extraordinarily accomplished people have grown up in difficult circumstances, and that many people who lack passion and fail to add to the world in positive ways have grown up in exceptional circumstances. If you water down your burning desires, you will get a soggy version of what you dreamed of.

YOUR UNITY WITH DIVINE INTELLIGENCE

Think of all the technological marvels that we sometimes take for granted! The Industrial Revolution of the 18th and 19th centuries promised to free humanity from having to work so hard so that we could apply ourselves to more creative and Spiritual pursuits. Indeed, machines did create a better way of life in many ways, with advancements in medicine, housing, education, and transportation. But technology has also created new and far more complex problems.

For example, taking a hot bath no longer requires laboriously heating and carrying water. But as our physical labor has decreased, our collective health has not achieved anything close to perfection. Cardiac disease has become a major problem in technological countries. Cancer was once a rare illness — most people didn't live long enough to get it — but now it is a leading cause of death. AIDS has been more or less brought under control in the United States for those who can tolerate the difficult and very expensive medications, but it is killing millions in Africa and Asia. How did we get to this strange place? The answer is intimately connected to the development of science, and specifically to the influence of one remarkable man.

Sir Isaac Newton is often described as the paradigm of rationality and nonmystical thinking. His *Mathematical Principles of Natural Philosophy*, published in 1687, used a coherent set of physical laws to explain everything that happens in the Universe. The *Principia*, as it was called, included descriptions of the laws of motion and theory of gravitation, both of which defined the course of scientific thought for the next two hundred years.

Isaac Newton was a superstar in his day. There was nowhere he could go without being recognized. But Newton's personality was shy and retiring — and not especially pleasant. He was a quiet professor at Cambridge when he wrote the *Principia*, with no intention of publishing it, but a friend of Newton's read the manuscript and rushed it into print. Almost overnight, Newton was declared a genius, the father of the scientific revolution, the seer of a whole new vision of the physical Universe. The Newtonian Revolution had an enormous impact not only on science, but on all levels of society, because his laws gave humankind the first unified theory that explained how everything works. In Newton's Universe, things happened like clockwork.

This vision of a clockwork Newtonian Universe came to encompass every human activity. In short order, the whole world was understood as a gigantic, carefully balanced machine. What's often overlooked is the fact that Newton himself was a renowned theologian and Spiritual thinker. In fact, Newton was one of the great <u>Alchemists</u> of his day.

Alchemy was a Spiritual discipline that gradually became more understood (or misunderstood) as only a physical and chemical process. However, for the true Alchemist, the transformation of base metals into gold symbolized the evolution of the human Spiritual organism into a higher form. Essentially, the Alchemists pursued Spiritual goals through material means. The ultimate goal of Alchemy was lifting humankind to a higher state of being.

As for Isaac Newton, he was not known for his beloved Alchemy, but for his rational materialism. Until the day he died, Newton the Alchemist was hailed as Newton "The Father of the Age of

Reason," and his ideas were accepted as absolute fact until 1905, when a Swiss patent clerk named Albert Einstein published his General Theory of Relativity — and everything changed all over again. Einstein's theory could not be contained within Newton's laws. Suddenly, the clockwork Universe had broken down.

The Theory of Relativity proposes that the characteristics of a phenomenon *are relative to the characteristics of the observer.* If you are standing still and watching a train go by, the train appears to be moving. However, if you are moving at the same speed as the train, in the same direction, the train appears to be standing still. Simple as this idea may seem, when applied to classical physics, it caused scientists to doubt everything they thought they knew about the Universe.

Newtonian physics had described light as a stream of energy radiating from a source. After Einstein, however, the nature of light became much less certain. Physicists first proved that light is made of <u>particles</u>. Then they proved that light is made of <u>waves</u>. Finally, scientists determined that light can be either particles or waves, <u>depending on the expectations of the observer.</u> So we can't really say <u>exactly</u> what light is — and this can be demonstrated by an experiment so simple it is regularly performed in school science fairs by children with only rudimentary science skills.

The shifting nature of light is only one example of what modern physics has wrought. There are many more: With his so-called "Uncertainty Principle," the

German physicist Werner Heisenberg proved that <u>it is impossible to know both the speed and the position of an electron at the same time</u>. If you fix the position, you cannot accurately measure the speed. If you accurately measure the speed, you lose the electron's position. The implications of the Uncertainty Principle have been applied to everything from stock market prediction to love and relationships. Moreover, science has demonstrated that atoms, the very building blocks of physical reality, are made up almost entirely of empty space. On the subatomic level, <u>matter is an illusion.</u>

GOOD VIBRATIONS

Pythagoras, the ancient Greek philosopher, compared the relationships of vibrating musical notes to the mathematical relationships of heavenly bodies in motion. Pythagoras' research, which culminated in his concept of the "Music of the Spheres," proposed an indescribable symphony of vibrations that permeated the Universe. "Indescribable" because the music of the spheres takes place in a dimension that humans cannot hear. Pythagoras' ethereal music was part of the fabric of the Universe — or, rather, it was the very fabric itself.

With this in mind, consider the latest attempt by theoretical physicists to create a "Unified Theory of Everything," which they call "String Theory." This begins with the question of what the most fundamental building blocks of the Universe actually look like. The ancient Greeks had correctly imagined tiny microscopic points, which they called "atoms." Modern scientists proved that the Greeks were right about atoms, but when they learned that there were particles even smaller than atoms, they just assumed that these subatomic particles were points, too.

According to String Theory, however, the smallest components that make up matter are actually tiny <u>strings</u>. Some of the strings are closed, like rubber bands, and some of them are open. The first reason that a string is better than a point is that, while a point can be in only one place at a time, a string is in effect <u>in more than one place at a time,</u> since it has length.

Also, the strings vibrate, the way a violin string vibrates, and the vibrations of the various strings <u>interact with each other</u>. Imagine a violin's strings. The sound made by plucking one string correlates to a particular vibrational frequency, or "note." Each note is what we think of as a subatomic particle. When two or more strings vibrate together, they create a harmony, which is two particles interacting. As harmonies build on each other, matter is generated. String Theory is saying that the substance that makes up our physical reality is generated by the harmonies of these strings vibrating together, like music.

Whenever two long strings cross each other, they exchange ends, or "intercommute," interweaving like the fibers in a Persian carpet. These fibers, however, are able to stretch to infinite lengths, which explains how two quarks on either side of the galaxy could communicate. The intercommunication of the strings shapes our physical reality. Physicists no longer have to imagine particles as tiny points sitting at a distance from each other in the fabric of space-time. There is no distance between anything in the Universe. *We Are All One.*

As String Theory resolves many of the inner conflicts of science, it reveals more and more of its Spiritual aspect. Consider the question of multiple dimensions. <u>Physicists have long theorized that in order for there to be matter in our Universe, there also has to be a sort of nonmatter, which in effect does not exist</u>. Although this was a difficult problem, it was an easy one for physicists to ignore until the theory of strings came along. For the new theory of strings to be a true unified theory, it had to include everything in the Universe, even matter that cannot be shown to exist! But there was a problem. If this nonmatter wasn't in our Universe, where was it? To find it, physicists had to apply an entirely new mathematical approach called "Supersymmetry." Supersymmetry solved the problem by showing that there is much, much more to the Universe than we previously thought.

Where we previously thought the Universe existed in four dimensions — three spatial dimensions plus the fourth dimension of time — Supersymmetry showed that in fact the Universe is made up of 10 dimensions! At the Big Bang, String Theory tells us, the 10 dimensions split into two connected sections, like a balloon squeezed in the middle: a six-dimensional Universe of an infinitely tiny size, and a four-dimensional Universe of an infinitely large size. Ours is the four-dimensional one.

The missing nonmatter does indeed exist, only we can't see it because it's in the six hidden dimensions. <u>So then if the matter in our Universe needs the nonmatter to exist, how do the two types of matter interact?</u> The answer lies in the fact that strings can stretch and intercommute with one another not only over infinite distances, but even over all 10 dimensions.

<u>So what does that mean for you?</u>

LIVING IN THE PAST, LIVING IN THE FUTURE

Before you became an atomic structure, you were unique energy and information. You had your own individual signature essence and particular distinctive *Resonance.* <u>Your unique essence has existed forever, exists now, and will always exist!</u>

At the very beginning of your physical life on this Earth, your first cell was a sphere. Our planet is also a sphere. A sphere is symbolic of diversity within Unity. Our cells radiate out, and resonate with each other, other life forms, our planet, and all other spherical planets. <u>We are literally One with the music of the spheres.</u>

Whatever it is that you are here to do and experience, know that you are one of a kind. There is no one like you, there never has been, and there never will be. Just as there are no two snowflakes alike, with their intricate symmetrical structure of crystals, you are an intricate symmetrical crystalline structure.

In the material aspect of our world, crystals have been used for the storage and transmission of energy in healing technology. Crystals also form the foundation for liquid crystal computer technology. Radio telescopes made with crystals are positioned all over our planet, as well as in satellites in space, capturing Universal *Resonance*, hundreds of light years away.

In our bodies, our crystals, nanosecond by nanosecond, receive and communicate with subtle layers and levels of Intelligence. Because our bodies are 70 percent water, we are literally like liquid crystal rivers of consciousness, connected to the *Quantum Hologram*, which is the wholeness behind all dimensions.

The same permanent Laws of Creation apply to the structure and function of every cell in our bodies. You embrace these permanent biophysical Laws of Creation to create perfect balance in each of your cells and all of your organ systems. You experience increased vitality, enhanced health and well-being. Your body becomes the beautiful temple in which you dwell. Each cell remains alive and vibrating with Life Force, intact in accordance with both the "Laws of the Material World" and unseen "Universal Laws."

Sound Health, Sound Wealth

Thoughts become things, and feelings and feeling-based faith provide the power — quantum energy propelling the thoughts and ideas to become your particular *Heart's Desires.* Through your *Future Memories* you create a literal magnetic attractor pattern of *Your Heart's Most Treasured Desires.*

As adults, we may sometimes find ourselves living in the past, reviewing old unfair situations — what we did that wasn't right, or what others did or didn't do to meet our needs. Or, we notice that we are thinking about the future — going over the list of things that it will take to make us happy: more money, the right partner, the perfect house. We do live in the physical world, so having enough to eat, a comfortable dwelling, and enough money to be comfortable is absolutely necessary and important. However, all the money and possessions in the world cannot guarantee us health, happiness, or the feeling states of peace and contentment. Even the "perfect" relationship cannot create what we need to accept and enjoy our innermost selves.

LIVING IN THE PRESENT MOMENT

Learning to live in the "present moment," a fairly difficult practice for most of us, can lead us to real gratitude for what we do have. The past is already behind us, and the future hasn't yet happened.

We can learn a lot about staying in the present moment from children. Most children live in the present moment, they believe in magic, and they believe that anything is possible. When children are playing with a favorite stuffed animal, or doll, they might have imaginary conversations in which they appear to be in a whole other reality. Yet if you were to ask a child, "Is your doll really talking to you?" he or she might answer the question by saying, "No." Children are able to perceive the consensus about present reality and simultaneously enjoy a mythical and magical world.

Adults who still believe in magic tend to be very intuitive and often nonjudgmental. They are able to tap into the invisible unseen *Realm of the Miraculous*, using their feeling-based thoughts to access other dimensions, bringing back extraordinary leaps of knowledge, breakthrough inventions, and fresh ways of understanding that *We Are All One*. Their thoughts, feelings, and Faith become things that enrich our world. Buddha, Plato, Jesus, great religious teachers, Madame Curie, Robert Thornton, Martin Luther King, Rosa Parks, Margaret Sanger, Franklin Delano Roosevelt, Mother Teresa, Nelson Mandela, Princess Diana, Helen Keller, Mahatma Gandhi, the Wright brothers, the Beatles, Karl Pribram — the list of people who have experienced and created paradigm shifts is very long.

PARADIGM SHIFTS

Extraordinary leaps in technology occur at an ever-increasing rate because human beings are able to reach into other dimensions to find the miraculous and put it into service on Earth. Computers and other forms of "artificial intelligence" are less artificial all the time. Not only do they act and respond in a binary code, they can pick up data from the ether without a human being specifically programming them to perform a function. I have a dear friend, Andrew, who is not programmed into my cell phone, nor am I in his. Sometimes his name, but not his phone number, will appear on the digital screen of my phone. It always happens when he is thinking of me, or I of him. When I respond to the graphic prompt and call him, I find that he has not physically taken the action of calling me. Both of our desires to connect with one another interact in the unseen energy and information of the *Quantum Hologram* and become expressed in physical form. The appearance of his name is a heart-based prompt for a physical connection, so I call him. I have since heard of several other people who have the same experience. It is both fascinating and heart-warming.

The creators of dramatic technological break-throughs have several things in common. They envisioned a specific outcome, added energetic fuel by using feelings and Faith, tapped into the *Quantum Hologram* and brought back to this Earth something that was extraordinary — something that changed the world. We all have the opportunity to change ourselves, recognize our true interaction with *The Realm of the Miraculous*, and bring back something — an idea, an invention, the daily practice that creates Sound Health and Sound Wealth.

As you consciously make new connections with the *Quantum Hologram,* you don't have to have big lottery wins (although you are more likely to!) or make huge changes in order to experience fulfillment. Very often it's the other way around. Instead of big leaps of being overwhelmed, <u>small graceful steps allow fulfillment in each present moment.</u>

When we are willing and able to properly utilize our intellect and feel a heart-based *Resonance* of exactly how it feels to be fulfilled, doors swing open, the Universe unfolds its mysteries and delivers its wisdom from sources known and unknown.

HOW TO CREATE A *FUTURE MEMORY*

Having a *Future Memory* is somewhat like sending an email. You type your message into your computer, and it's encrypted into binary electronic packets of light. When you send the message, its minute bits journey independently through the Web, wandering from server to server, until they reach their destination, where they spontaneously reassemble, by themselves, into a whole, coherent message. The photons of this message first scatter in chaos, and then reassemble into wholeness. Your email traveled at the "speed of light." Although an oversimplification, your email is like writing a letter, tearing it up, letting the wind blow it in a congruent direction, and having it show up to the receiver intact!

Because there is no intermediary, your *Future Memories* actually travel <u>faster</u> than the speed of light. When you transmit your *Future Memory* into the *Quantum Hologram* with focus and intention, you can't help receiving back at least a thousandfold. Just as we program computers, we can program the *Quantum Hologram* to communicate back to us through meaningful synchronicities. This is possible for each and every one of us; this is our Divine Inheritance. This Divine energetic connection is where all things are known and understood. You can set your heart-based intention to connect with, and receive from, this vast sea of unlimited energy information and infinite possibilities. By using heart-based intentions to create *Future Memories*, you partner with the *Realm of the Miraculous*. You become your own "Spontaneous Fulfillment Center."

Creating *Future Memories* is a powerful technique for bringing about specific desired outcomes in our lives. Your powerful Subconscious Mind has a different relationship to time than does your Conscious Mind. Your Subconscious Mind is literal, almost childlike, and performs all functions in present moment only. By giving high *Resonance*, heart-based directives to your Subconscious Mind, you can positively affect your own metabolic physical feeling states and health by connecting with endless support from dimensions beyond space and time, support from the *Realm of the Miraculous.*

To create your *Future Memories*, first find a comfortable place in which you have privacy and will not be interrupted. Then, in your journal, make a list of every word that you can think of that describes a feeling. Although there are hundreds, if not thousands, of words in the English language that describe feelings, there are really only eight basic emotions. These same eight basic emotions are found in all cultures and sub-cultures, across history: Sadness, Happiness, Surprise, Anger, Confusion, Fear, Disgust, and Hurt. All other feelings are blends of the eight basic emotions. Envy is a blend of anger and fear. Contempt is a blend of anger and disgust. Joy is an intense state of happiness. Excitement is a blend of happiness and anticipatory surprise.

You may find some feelings more negative; others may appear more neutral; some will seem more positive. All feelings provide us with important information. <u>All feelings and emotions developed because they were critical to our survival as a species. For these reasons it is imperative that we be able to correctly identify all feeling states so we never release all of any feeling, even the ones we find the most noxious, so that we can always recognize all feelings. This is for our healthy survival. In addition, we need to have ways to quickly release negative feelings once they are identified so that we can avoid traveling in toxic loops of unproductive feeling states.</u>

You can release or diminish the intensity of all feelings through any physical exercise: This might take the form of walking, stretching, dancing. You may also release feelings by using imagery: for example, creating a sturdy container in your mind's eye, into which you put the feelings you wish to release. Using movement, or imagery, or your own particular method, consciously release 90 percent of the feelings you no longer need or want into the molten core of the Earth, where they will be immediately transformed into energy that is positive and life giving. Use intention and mindfulness in this process. We need to keep some amount of each feeling so that we can accurately identify all feelings, both in ourselves and in others. This ability is essential to our very survival.

Again, in your journal, create a daily *Feeling Inventory*. Take a few minutes at the end of the day to put a check by any feeling you experienced that day. You will discover that in only a few days, you become more aware of exactly what you are feeling. As you review your *Feeling Inventory* over a period of weeks, look for patterns — feelings that you avoid and feelings that you feel frequently. Notice that as you acknowledge and release feelings that may be unpleasant or too intense, you create more space for life-enhancing emotions.

In order to experience your most positive dreams, you might say to yourself: *"I feel heart Resonance for my most precious dreams. My heart-based feeling technology, already installed within me and connected with Divine Intelligence, creates, <u>Now</u>, the actual experience of exactly how it feels to live my dreams. I feel relaxed and calm, as well as excited, because my* *dreams are realized. I feel it now."* With focus and repetition, your intention becomes programmed into your powerful Subconscious Mind!

On a continuing basis, practice creating states of positive feeling: peace, joy, compassion, excitement, curiosity, relaxation, love, and satisfaction. Use both memory and future imagination to ignite these states. As you become accustomed to this, you will very quickly be able to go "in state." You will have the <u>feeling experience</u> of your dreams in an instant.

Sound Health, Sound Wealth

Chapter Three

The Principle of Your Magical Divine Experiment ™

In a world where we are continually instructed to set goals and take massive physical actions for the achievement of those goals, it is my pleasure to share with you new ways in which <u>you can achieve more by actually doing less</u>. You become the *Resonance* of that which you wish to achieve, Body, Mind, and Spirit. *Resonance* is, in fact, the foundation of *Your Magical Divine Experiment*™.

The fulfillment of *Your Heart's Most Treasured Desires* is expressed from within yourself to create the manifestation of your most precious dreams in the world outside of yourself. This takes place in the comfort of your overstuffed armchair, in front of the warm glow of the fire, on the beach, or in your own special sacred place.

Physical action is most effective when we have first been magnetically and magically drawn into the creative and passionate energy field of our *Heart's Desires*. We are then inspired, guided, and supported by synchronistic events and universal clues that illuminate and clarify our experiences, turning our life's paths into a joyous treasure hunt. Whatever it is we wish to become, experience, and achieve is more easily accomplished when we have been invited into the energetic fields of opportunity.

Each of us comes into the world at a specific point in our Spiritual development. As we make progress in our *Magical Divine Experiment*, our lives expand and increase in perfect *Resonance*.

How much positive energy are you able to share with other people? Are you reactive or proactive when obstacles appear? Do you have enough inner strength to face the challenges that make real growth possible? Or do you back away from difficulties that seem just too overwhelming?

And once you've reached a certain level, what can motivate you to the next one? If your life already seems full and blessed — with family, good health, finances, career, and creative self intact — what is the source of desire for still further development?

The purpose of this chapter is to illuminate the impact our human awareness has on the energetic interchanges between the subatomic particles of our physical and biological selves and the vast omnipotent ocean of consciousness and intelligence. These interchanges provide the inspiration, passion, and direction that are unique and correct for you, and you alone. Together, we will use our knowledge of this process as the foundation for *Your Magical Divine Experiment*.

THOUGHTS, FEELINGS, AND ACTIONS BECOME PHYSICAL REALITIES

In order to create the most magical process and results in the least possible amount of time, we need to become exquisitely aware of how to harness our thoughts and feelings to expedite our exciting journey. *The Law of Attraction* we use is not bound by the physical laws of the Earth's magnetics. *The Law of Attraction* is universal and operates non-locally through the *Quantum Hologram.* This magnetic power of the *Law of Attraction* does not diminish over physical distance, space, or time. As we increasingly master our perceptions, beliefs, and thought/feeling patterns, we magnetically attract that which we most desire. This process requires Faith, that is, confidence, trust, and belief that is not based on existing proof. In order to be where we want to be and feel the way we want to feel, we have to let go of our attachments to how this process unfolds. We develop and use Faith to step aside and let synchronicity magically open doors, often in mysterious ways.

Old thoughts, beliefs, and ideas of lack and limitation are actual neurochemical pathways on a cellular level. These habitual patterns can create both emotional and molecular impediments to new opportunities and ideas. By changing your internal dialogue — that is, the thoughts and feelings on which you focus — you can actually create your own new biochemistry of hope. These endorphins of hope and bliss enhance your awareness and creativity. You become more aware, open, and receptive to opportunities you may have overlooked.

The truth is, we are surrounded by countless creative thoughts, feelings, and opportunities every minute of every day. Many fables and stories teach about the wanderer who made lifelong, exhausting, unproductive physical journeys through the harsh wilderness, only to find that the precious treasure he sought had been buried in his own back yard all along.

Exploring your energetic opportunities isn't primarily a matter of where you are. <u>Who</u> you are is infinitely more important, and does not depend on or require an actual geographic change. *Your Life's Purpose* and the means to express it — all your most precious dreams — are within you right now, awaiting expression.

At this moment, this *Parenthesis in Eternity*, most of us are aware that the acquisition of material things will not, in itself, create the feelings we desire. Wealth in the form of money does, however, make more options available: more time to create, have fun, relax, and nurture and sustain our relationships; more opportunities for travel, reading, and hobbies; and greater capabilities for helping those less fortunate. Buckminster Fuller, in the 1950s, estimated that there were enough resources in the world for each and every man, woman, and child to have at least $4 million per person. With the advances in technology, agriculture, and manufacturing, and the enormous accomplishments of medical science in effectively treating and containing illness and disease that historically took the lives and well-being of millions, imagine what that figure might be today.

So, it still isn't that there aren't enough resources to provide abundance for everyone. The problem is, the resources have not been uniformly available. There has been a mistaken belief in life as a "zero-sum game": what is given to you must have been taken away from me. But just as a candle can light another and another without its own light being diminished, *True Wealth* in every form can and must be shared. We now know that the needs of all can be met without detriment to any.

A simple and eloquent teaching that expresses this idea: "One can't go home until we all go home." Strengthening your ability to manifest abundance directly impacts fear-based boundaries on a macro scale — and assists in healing individual, community, and planetary distress. Imagine if every man, woman, child — all living creatures — had more than their basic life needs met. Each sentient being would then have more time, energy, and motivation to experience and express their own magical and purposeful harmony with all that is. When the cup of plenty overflows for each and for all, poverty consciousness ceases to exist.

MICHAEL AND JENNIFER'S
MAGICAL DIVINE EXPERIMENT

Michael and Jennifer had already been friends for years when they found themselves spending more time together. Friendship grew into love. They were in their mid-thirties, and had almost given up the dream of finding the right life partner. They knew each other's strengths and flaws, and their relationship was grounded in reality. Still, they overflowed at their blessed union. They crafted a simple and lovely ceremony on the beach with family and friends, and moved to the beautiful Northern California coast to live their dreams. Extremely undercapitalized, but with great hopes and dreams, they put a down payment on a beautiful old home. Their house perched on the top of a hill, in full sun, surrounded by majestic redwoods.

Michael and Jennifer dreamed of creating a successful business together. Michael was artistic, creative — a magician with his hands — able to build almost anything. Jennifer had been a university fiscal officer, with virtuoso computer skills. After researching small-business opportunities, they decided to open a graphic sign business.

Michael was a musician and had once traded guitar lessons for training with a friend who owned a successful sign business. He had learned the basics — painting, building, and pricing — and the appropriate materials for different kinds of signs. He had done signage during his high school years to generate extra income. Jennifer learned how to master computer sign equipment, layout, and design. She was already a great designer. The newlyweds believed that if they

Three
The Principle of
Your Magical
Divine
Experiment ™

100

could stay focused and balanced, and keep their "eye on the prize," they would create a fulfilling, thriving enterprise.

Michael and Jennifer took their small savings, and leased a 1000-square-foot warehouse/shop. They were nervous and excited when they signed the three-year lease for their new shop, which also required a $2,000 security deposit They had just under $5,000 left, and still needed cash to buy signage materials and pay for their living expenses. They were in a very precarious financial situation. Things just had to work out.

Of course, Jen and Michael were nervous. They knew that they had to find creative, innovative ways to get orders, since there were already three successful sign shops in town. They simply did not have the budget to cover splashy yellow-page ads, or even small ads in the local newspaper.

Michael was an explorer. He discovered a beautiful trail in the redwoods, bordered by exotic white and purple wild orchids, that led down to the ocean. It was there that he began to meditate and practice his Future Memories. As he listened to the crashing waves, he breathed in the moist ocean air. He imagined in full color detail exactly how it would feel to have a successful business. He and Jennifer would enjoy abundant cash flow, celebrate creative freedom, and eventually be able to travel. Michael's Future Memories also included cherished elements of his present life: daily exercise at the beach or in the redwoods, delicious and nourishing food, time to relax and have fun every day by himself, with new friends and business acquaintances, and with Jen.

Sound Health, Sound Wealth

Without really thinking about it, Michael expanded his Energetic Boundaries, mapping out his part of the due diligence. He intuitively knew that the omnipotent Divine Intelligence — the Quantum Hologram — *would orchestrate the plan. He just had to specify his energetic intentions and hold to them. Michael wrote down the specific amount of money they would attract each month for the next year. He knew he would give equal exchange of Life Force, by creating beautifully crafted signs for the specific needs of each of his clients. He also committed to donating four hours a week to helping those in need.*

Michael had almost no experience in the sign business, but he did have plenty of experience in attracting and projecting positive energy. He had always offered outstanding service at every job he ever had, based on his awareness that carefully tended positive relationships are the foundation for success in every area of life.

He had learned that the Universal Infinite Intelligence that interacts with all life forms must be accessed through faith and perseverance. He knew that to activate this cosmic alliance he would need to specify his intentions through each and every thought, word, and deed. He knew that faith without action was not enough. If he applied action-based faith, and stuck with his Divine Experiment, miracles would arrive when he least expected them.

Michael had overcome many challenges in his life. The most difficult were his genetic and childhood legacies — his conscious and unconscious beliefs about lack and limitation. He believed that if someone had more, someone else would

Three
The Principle of
Your Magical
Divine
Experiment ™

102

automatically have less. His unconscious beliefs had kept him struggling financially in his twenties. His father had been a successful businessman whose health had steadily declined with overwork, stress, alcohol, and eventually, a failed marriage. His father also believed that "Life is all work and no play." He constantly reminded his children that "Money doesn't grow on trees."

Michael and Jen didn't have the money to advertise in the conventional ways, so they looked at the paper each day at the various business notices. They knew that new businesses might need signs. Jennifer created a bright-blue, elegant flier, offering customized free estimates, fast turnaround, and a free door-to-door service. They sent out about 20 fliers per week, selecting the recipients together.

Michael wrote a heartfelt personalized note on each flier, wishing the new business owner great success in his or her business. After he completed each note, Michael took the time to envision each recipient as spectacularly successful — as successful as he wanted his own business to be. Before placing the fliers in the mail, each carrying a beautiful purposefully selected postage stamp, Michael blessed each flier and blissfully imagined the surprise, delight, peace, harmony, joy, and abundance his new customers would experience.

One rainy afternoon, however, Michael noticed he was feeling fearful and discouraged. He was walking from business to business, trying to promote his own new enterprise. But before he could even introduce himself, the people in charge held up their hands and indicated that he was not welcome, pointing to signs that read, "No solicitors."

Three
The Principle of
Your Magical
Divine
Experiment ™

103

With the mortgage payment and the office rent both due, Michael wondered what he and Jen had been thinking when they moved to a new city without larger savings to cushion them. He and Jen had been so sure everything would work out. They had so much faith in themselves, each other, and their plan. They had absolutely believed that Divine Intelligence had inspirited them to create this new life together.

Soaking wet, Michael entered a coffee and tea shop that felt toasty warm and cozy. He drank in the exquisite rich aroma. He ordered a cup of African red bush tea, doctored it with two spoonfuls of organic clover honey, and picked out a small oak table in the corner. As it happened, there was a bookshelf beside the table filled with old paperbacks. Michael picked one out; it was called Think and Grow Rich. Opening a page at random, Michael began to read. "No man is ever whipped unless he quits in his own mind."

"Is this an accident?" Michael wondered. "If it is, it's coming at exactly the right time. "He read about the temporary defeats of people like Henry Ford and the Wright brothers. Phrases leaped off the page. "A quitter never wins and a winner never quits." "Every adversity, every failure, and every heartache carries with it the seed of an equivalent or greater benefit."

Michael took a deep breath, opened his wallet, and reverently removed his Magical Divine Template™ that he and Jennifer had written for their new business; it read: "Michael and Jennifer now enjoy their wonderfully fulfilling business. They net a minimum of three thousand dollars per month after all bills, tithes, and taxes are paid. They provide excel-

Three
The Principle of
Your Magical
Divine
Experiment™

104

lent, timely service, create elegant, substantial products, and attract enthusiastic customers who love and appreciate their work. Each new customer refers a friend or acquaintance within 30 days of the receipt of their sign."

Michael smiled and changed his breathing. He exhaled tension, worry, anxiety, and fear. He consciously breathed in optimism, hope, faith, joy, relief, peace, inspiration, excitement, and gratitude. In two minutes he had completely changed his physiology. He put an authentic sparkle in his eyes. He envisioned and felt himself, Jennifer, and their appreciative loyal new customers enjoying their beneficial association.

When he returned to his shop, he discovered that another meaningful coincidence had occurred. Jennifer had also been feeling anxious about the viability of their business. Just about the time Michael had entered the coffee shop, she had remembered to take out and read her Template. She, too, had created and felt the images of success in her whole being: Body, Mind, and Spirit. Just as she finished, Jennifer felt peace and calm come over her. She said a prayer of thanks.

The bell on the door chimed as a man entered. He was from the local Navy base and was interested in ordering over a thousand signs that would showcase their recent remodel. He needed immediate delivery, as the contracted sign maker had, just that morning, defaulted. The Naval representative was still there going over the architectural plans with Jennifer, when Michael returned.

The next day, Michael and Jennifer drove through the beautiful summer countryside and presented the bid they had *prepared for the Navy. It was accepted that very day. They had their first $20,000 order!*

Michael and Jennifer's business netted $80,000 in the first year. The next year they had exclusive customers and could hardly keep up with all the orders. They hired sign painters who had tremendous experience, from other shops that weren't as busy. Their success was exponential.

Michael and Jennifer achieved abundance in less than four years. They sold their business when Jennifer became pregnant with their first child.

Michael continued working for the new owners for a year, as agreed on in his contract of sale, while he created his new consulting business. Michael applied the same dynamic principles they had used with the sign-making business to his extremely successful consulting business. He Made a Decision, *created his* Future Memories, *with the specific details of his desired outcomes, fleshing out a* Divine Experiment *that used energetic principles to propel his "Internal blueprint" into success. He continued to use faith and willingness to let the outcome unfold as he followed the synchronistic clues to success.*

Three
The Principle of
Your Magical
Divine
Experiment ™

106

REMOVING BARRIERS TO OUR HEART'S DESIRES
From Toxic Anxiety, Free-Floating Anxiety, and Fear, to Sacred Anxiety

Fear and anxiety are the most profound impediments we face in bringing Sound Heath and Sound Wealth into our lives. Fear has been defined as "a deeply distressing emotion, aroused by impending danger, evil, or pain, whether the threat is real or imagined." Whether the unusual noise outside our home is an indicator of actual lurking danger, or only a raccoon rummaging in the trash, we take actions to be on the safe side. This way, we are protected. We appropriately experience the unpleasant emotion of fear as an incentive to "do something." The ability to feel, identify, and correctly react to fear can be critical to our survival as individuals, the survival of our loved ones, and the very survival of our species. You are alive and reading this book because your ancestors, far and near, accurately recognized the emotion of fear, responded appropriately to the perceived threat, and were able to do what was necessary to survive.

Anxiety, on the other hand, is "distress or uneasiness caused by fear of danger or misfortune." Anxiety is caused by the anticipation of impending danger, not by danger itself. Anxiety is a "second-order feeling" — it is not critical to survival, although it may feel that way. Anxiety is not fear. Fear is the immediate physiologically driven survival response to perceived danger. Anxiety is a response to thoughts, feelings, and imagination.

There is a complex neurobiology of fear and anxiety. Cortisol, for example, is a stress hormone created by our bodies to deal with emergency and life-threatening occurrences. Norepinephrine is a vasoconstrictor that can bring on a variety of sleep and anxiety disorders. Adrenaline, produced by the kidneys, is a

Three
The Principle of
Your Magical
Divine
Experiment ™

107

vasodilator that creates rapid delivery of all hormones, increased heart rate, and extraordinary physical strength. Excessive production of cortisol can suppress adrenaline production, weakening physical, emotional, and Spiritual immunity. <u>With constantly increasing stress, we often mistake anxiety for fear. The resulting increased presence of cortisol affects our every thought, word, feeling, and deed.</u>

So-called "free-floating anxiety" is more and more present in our own individual lives, and more and more pervasive in our shared global experience. Free-floating anxiety may envelop you seemingly out of nowhere. Your kids are okay; your basic needs are met. By most standards, you should feel secure and happy, but perhaps you don't. Free-floating anxiety is that inauspicious feeling that "the other shoe is going to drop."

Surprisingly, some people feel most anxious when things are going well. When success is achieved, sometimes some strange things start to happen. Some people become afraid. A comparison might be that you've learned the secret of flight from some amazing wizard. You start flapping your arms, and the next thing you know, you're high up in the air. At that point, your mind starts to play some tricks. You start thinking about what an amazing thing this is. Then you wonder how long it can go on. That leads to doubt that it will go on very much longer, maybe not for even another second. And that, of course, is when you start to fall.

Three
The Principle of
Your Magical
Divine
Experiment ™

108

The same chain of thought can accompany success. People start to back off. They start saying things like, "I just want to be comfortable. I just want to put bread on the table. I just want to be free from worry about how I'm going to pay the bills." They don't want material and Spiritual abundance anymore. They're ready to settle for a lot less. In the moment it seems to generate less fear.

Magical Consciousness is very different. Magical Consciousness means, "I'm grateful for what has come into my life, and I look forward with certainty to what is yet to come. So let it flow!" Magical Consciousness sees every day and even every moment as a "new beginning."

When we start feeling anxiety that failure is somehow inevitable, we're seeing the world with limited consciousness. Regardless of the size of our bank accounts, we're still thinking with limitation. We set a goal for ourselves, achieve it, and then believe it would be greedy to expect anything more. Not true! The more we receive, the more we can share — so there's nothing greedy about it. We can then proceed to the next level.

HALT

Free-floating anxiety may derive from energy and information floating around in the collective consciousness of the world, or even in the microcosm of your neighborhood, workplace, or home. Free-floating

Three
The *Principle* of
Your *Magical*
Divine
Experiment™

109

anxiety may also be connected with your personal psyche, providing you with information about lingering conscious or subconscious issues that may be impeding your progress. It may be that there is something that you have not yet had the strength or comfort level to deal with. We are more likely to be vulnerable to states of anxiety when we are hungry, angry, lonely, or tired: The acronym is <u>HALT.</u> HALT is a signal to stop and provide ourselves with the resources we need — food, emotional support, rest, and sleep. This is the time to call on our own support system and also consider connecting with the wisdom of a skilled health care professional, counselor, or psychotherapist.

Anxiety is more than just a word. In the 21st century, it's a basic element of our lives. People take anxieties for granted. Sometimes we're even proud of them. President Harry Truman once said, "If you can't take the heat, get out of the kitchen," and many of us have this attitude about the pressures we live with.

Yet there's no doubt that anxiety is counterproductive to success, and certainly to true prosperity. So, aside from the need to seem like a hero, why do we put up with it? Even more important, why do we experience it in the first place? How do we process it? Can we get rid of it — or, if we can't, is there any way that the enormous energy of work-related stress can work for us rather than against us?

Three
The Principle of
Your Magical
Divine
Experiment ™

110

Imagine two people who experience the same work environment day in and day out. They might be partners in a small business, or they could be colleagues of equal rank in a large corporation. Both are living with serious amounts of pressure. Yet one of these people feels motivated by the demands of the situation, while the other is exhausted. How does this come to be?

Stress is just stress, isn't it? Why do some people experience it as a force pushing them forward, while others feel that stress is holding them back, if not bringing them to a stop altogether? At its very essence, anxiety is energy. It is our individual choice to learn ways in which we can focus and use this energy for our highest and best: Body, Mind, and Spirit. Yoga classes, walks in nature, moderate exercise, breathing, meditating, and praying are among the many ways to refocus and recycle "toxic anxiety" into "Sacred Anxiety." Identifying and interrupting the pattern of anxiety is key to accomplishing this idea.

Magical Consciousness teaches that the *Quantum Hologram* itself can be a source of anxiety. We may believe that stress is pain, pure and simple. But consider the possibility that what we experience as pain might be our inner resistance to growth. When that growth has finally taken place, the pain will be gone — just as the things that stressed us out at earlier points in our lives now seem perfectly manageable.

When we experience anxiety, we sometimes find ourselves caught in seemingly endless loops of dis-

Three
The Principle of
Your Magical
Divine
Experiment ™

111

tress. There is also, however, a feeling that I call "Sacred Anxiety," characterizing circumstances in which we can move into action — both physically and spiritually — to deal effectively with the situation. If you don't like your job, for example, or if your company is downsizing and you are concerned that your job will be cut, you can create a *Divine Action Plan.* You can imagine <u>how you want to feel in your new job or enterprise</u>; you create the "feeling state" first. Then you may update your résumé, check out possible job openings in your field, identify the resources for retraining or using your skills and experience in another field, obtain information about grants and training programs that would support your expansion and change, network with all your contacts, meet with an experienced vocational consultant, and, perhaps most importantly, connect with Divine Intelligence and open yourself to the unexpected synchronicities that will emerge around you. You can be assured that they will emerge, when you provide the internal environment in which that can happen.

FIRST AND SECOND THOUGHTS AND FEELINGS

It's simply a law of Nature that you cannot control your first thought and first feeling in response to a person or situation. You may be introduced to a new employee from another department in your company. If the new employee's voice seems loud and commanding to you, your first feeling may be discomfort,

Three
The Principle of
Your Magical
Divine
Experiment ™

112

or resentment. Your first thought may be, "She looks awfully young to be the assistant director of such an important division of the company." You may not be proud of that thought, but you need to accept it for what it is. But while you can't choose your first thought or your first feeling, you can choose your second thought and your second feeling through self-observation and the use of free will.

If you are tracking your thoughts and feelings in the moment, or, more likely, later on, you can choose to change your first feeling of discomfort to a second, more positive feeling, such as curiosity or interest.

You may conclude that the new employee was upset, and construct an empathic explanation of why her voice seemed inappropriately loud to you. On reflection, you may change your first thought to: "I wonder what her story is — how such an apparently young person qualified for such an important position."

In expanding our lives and our consciousness, it's important to track our own internal world of thoughts and feelings. We need to become exquisitely aware of any negative untrue thoughts and feelings we may direct toward ourselves. You may be at the end of the workday, reviewing your "To Do" list. If you weren't able to complete everything on the list, your first feeling may be guilt and your first thought may be, "Look at all the things I didn't get accomplished today." It is crucial for your own well-being that you be able to notice your first thought and feeling. If you are aware of your first thought and feeling, you can make a quick assessment of what was reasonable to accomplish that day. You can then use free will to create your second thought: "Look at all the things I accomplished today — maybe I need to make my 'To Do' lists more realistic." Your second feeling might be relief and satisfaction.

Use your connection with Divine Intelligence to rise to the occasion of creating your second thoughts and your second feelings. When you do this, you will be assisted to rise above your very human impulses, often caused by fear and anxiety, and to transcend subtle and not so subtle stereotypes about yourself and others. You move out of superficial judgment of yourself and others, into the high frequency *Resonance* of love and compassion, of Sound Health and Sound Wealth.

CREATING *YOUR UNIQUE* MAGICAL DIVINE EXPERIMENT™

Once again, find a comfortable place in which to sit and write. Make sure you have privacy and will not be interrupted. Identify situations in your life in which you seem to repeat the same dissatisfying behaviors over and over. Make a separate list for your Body, Mind, and Spirit. Take the right amount of time to create a list of the most significant areas that bother you, whether in Body, Mind, or Spirit. There may be areas in your life where you have been trapped for a long time. There might be problematic areas for you that are more recent, yet just as troublesome. Be as honest as you can be. This list is for your eyes only. You can often find clues about where you are trapped as you observe the most recurrent thoughts and feelings that resurface, time and time again.

For example, dissatisfaction with respect to your body may appear as a first thought like this: "I'm too fat and too lazy to eat right and exercise. This is an endless battle that I will never win." This thought may carry with it the first feelings of being helpless, discouraged, disappointed, depressed, ashamed, alone, and powerless.

You can't always choose your first thought or feeling, but you can choose your second thought and feeling. You can choose to think: *"I am radiantly healthy and vibrantly energetic. Every day and in every way the innate Intelligence of the cells of my being creates perfect balance and harmony in the temple of my being."*

Mentally, you may feel trapped by the thought that you have no funds for retirement. Your first thought might be: "I'll have to work for the rest of my life, while everybody else is traveling, gardening, and having fun." Your first feelings might be anxiety, worry, helplessness, resentfulness, jealousy, depression, aloneness.

Your second thought might be: *"I love what I do and I do what I love. I am open and receptive to rich abun-*

dance in all areas of my life, which flows to me now from sources known and unknown. I enjoy freedom and peace in ways I had never imagined. I stop 'Busy Mind' in one second. I simply say the word 'Stop!' and exhale. Busy Mind disappears. I now network with those who know my talent and experience, and I am creating a new business that will bring me all the money I want and need, now."

Your second feelings might be joy, excitement, contentment, peace, and relief.

Spiritually, you might be asking, "What kind of God allows a world where children are dying and there are those of us who try to solve problems by wars?" Your first feelings might be anger, frustration, sadness, fear, hopelessness, and disappointment.

Your second thought might be: *"Love is the unifying principle of the Universe. Love envelops the world: person by person, country by country. I choose the Resonance of love and compassion, knowing that others, in this exact moment, are also choosing the Resonance of love and compassion. All those who resonate with fear, judgment, rage, and violence are overcome by one person who chooses the energetic Resonance of compassion and love."*

Your second feelings might be relief, contentment, and acceptance.

Now give yourself permission to accept your first thought and your first feeling, over which you really have no control. You can choose your second thought and your second feeling through self-observation and the use of *Free Will.*

Three
The Principle of
Your Magical
Divine
Experiment ™

116

CREATING
YOUR MAGICAL DIVINE TEMPLATE™

*"You cannot have a heart's desire without
also having the means to fulfill it."*
— Dr. Emmett Fox

Creating a *Divine Template* is simply writing down
Your Heart's Most Treasured Desires on a small card, from
your journal or notebook. On it, you can write your
dreams, desires, and goals, one or more for each area
of your life, Body, Mind, and Spirit.

* How do you want to feel in your body, your
  emotions, your Spiritual life?

* What kind of relationships do you want in your
  life?

* What creative outlet appeals to you? (Painting,
  sculpting, writing a book or a poem?) Perhaps
  you have a nearly forgotten childhood dream.
  Allow yourself time to explore your former feelings and dreams and create new ones. Be audacious! (To the extent, of course, that you can
  learn to believe that what you desire can manifest
  into your life!)

* How do you want to generate the income? How
  do you want to attract Life Force in the form of
  money? What specific amounts?

Three
The Principle of
Your Magical
Divine
Experiment™

117

Sound Health, Sound Wealth

Even if your goal seems impossible or far off in the distance, if it is what you really want, *Make a Decision* that you will somehow attract wonderful and positive experiences into your life. You will be assisted from forces "seen" and "unseen."

"Breathe Light" into *Your Magical Divine Experiment!* Your goals and dreams may change along the way as synchronicity delivers you new choices and opportunities, perhaps in ways you have not yet imagined. You can leave the details of the manifestation process up to a *Power Greater Than Yourself.* With *Your Divine Template,* you are putting this request into the *Divine Intelligence* of the *Quantum Hologram.*

Here are some examples that might stimulate your imagination:

I, _____, am Now radiantly healthy, vibrantly energetic, lean, muscular, and strong. I am attracted to foods, people, places, and things that assist me to stay effortlessly focused on my well-being. I am happy, joyous, and free, Now!

I, _____, am Now attracted to foods that nourish, rejuvenate, and energize my whole being.

I, _____, Now am surrounded in loving, harmonious relationships. I am loving and compassionate toward myself and all others. I receive back compassion, understanding, and love from all others exponentially! I am filled with hope, faith, and creativity.

Every day, and in every way, my life is filled with exciting synchronistic events.

I, _____, Now enjoy wonderful opportunities, rich experiences, and Divine intervention in all areas of my life. I am filled with faith, joy, and hope, Now.

I, _____, Now enjoy what I do, and I do what I love. Life Force in the form of money comes to me as a result of integrity, honesty, love, and service. All my work is play; I never work another day.

Three
The *Principle* of
Your *Magical*
Divine
Experiment ™

119

Sound Health, Sound Wealth

Chapter Four

The *Principle* of *Energetic Boundaries:*
The Power of 'No'

What if you could feel even more energetic, enthusiastic, and passionate? What if you could more effortlessly draw from your reservoir of boundless energy, enjoying more passion, clarity, creativity, love, and Life Force, in all its pleasing forms? What if you could have more fun, feel less guilty and anxious, and be more competent and effective, with less effort?

By using the *Power of "No,"* you may delightfully assist yourself and those around you to create more sparkling vitality in your lives.

Not surprisingly, the word *no* has lots of negative connotations — and the dictionary's definition bears this out. *No* is defined as "a negative, expressing dissent, denial, or refusal." However, fully experiencing Sound Health and Sound Wealth means saying "Yes" to "No" under appropriate circumstances. Saying "No" can be necessary and healthy, for your own well-being and for that of others. A well-considered "No" can be a powerful "Yes" to your own essence, to your own needs, and to your own life's purpose.

Four
The Principle of
Energetic
Boundaries

121

'No' to All Toxins

No doubt you already take steps to shield yourself and your loved ones from toxic situations and environments. Whenever possible, you protect your food and water supply from toxic chemicals and contaminants. In the same way, creating appropriate "energetic boundaries" will protect your innermost self from toxicity.

Absorbing fear-based energy from others, getting caught in a feedback loop of negative thoughts and feelings, is physically, emotionally, and Spiritually depleting. When you feel anxious, fearful, or overly excited, adrenaline and cortisol are released into your bloodstream. This affects all other hormonal secretions, causing fatigue, exhaustion, and increased immune system vulnerability. The acid-alkaline balance in your body is altered, creating an internal environment of increased anxiety, depression, confusion, fear, and hopelessness. You lose vitality, and the reason is simple: You're literally <u>leaking energy.</u>

Energy Leaks

"Energy leaks" occur when you consciously or unconsciously give away time, thought, emotion, money, assistance, or any other valuable aspect of yourself in a way that is costly for your well-being and not truly helpful in the long run to anyone else.

You may have a neighbor, for example, or a co-worker, or a friend who repeatedly asks you for help with the same list of problems. After a time, you may notice that you feel frustrated, irritated, sad, or fatigued. It is important to establish appropriate energetic force fields in these situations so that you don't diminish your own power, thereby decreasing your own emotional and physical immune functions. Over time, you may actually begin to feel numb, unaware of the energy you're losing, unaware of the people and situations that drain your energy. You may be unaware of giving away your precious Life Force, because your behavior has become so habitual.

Fortunately, as the saying goes, "There is another way ..."

Gregg was a computer whiz who thrived on solving the mystery of how and why systems malfunctioned. He also loved learning about the diverse businesses that his company serviced: manufacturers of organic baby food, creators of complex websites, Internet galleries of gifted artists. Gregg did his best work listening to NPR in the background. He relished hearing the rich variety of audio presentations: new authors, debate teams, archeologists, political commentators, and, especially, music of all kinds.

Gregg didn't like to participate in the small-minded criticism and "Ain't it awful" conversations that sometimes went on in the staff room. He was well aware that "innocent" comments about other people's issues and struggles could sometimes result in hurt feelings and sullied reputations. Gregg's marriage had ended, but he had taken the "high road" in his divorce and refused to belittle or say negative things about his ex-wife. Throughout the process of separation, Gregg sometimes heard untrue negative comments about himself, his wife, and their marriage that hurt his feelings and made him feel angry. But he made a conscious effort not to let his anger drain his energy.

Gregg liked to have genuine relationships and not just "shoot the breeze" about nothing, or mindlessly criticize. One major factor in his ascendance to "rising star" status in his firm was that he always took a courageous stance about "tale bearing" at work. His usual response was that probably nobody had the real story and that <u>words can and do hurt people unnecessarily</u>. If the negative talk continued, he simply left the room.

Gregg taught by example. He refused to participate in nasty energy leaks and was willing to risk the criticism of the group in order to do what he knew was right.

Group pressure can be formidable and intimidating to most of us. Many of us have found ourselves remaining silent in situations where it would have been healthier, albeit more difficult, to say something to preserve healthy boundaries and maintain the "innocent until proven guilty" standard.

Energy leaks stop when you establish clear and appropriate energetic boundaries, a force field to safeguard you from the negative vibrations of other people and situations. You can create these boundaries by envisioning a positive electromagnetic energy field all around you. Your might wear a beautiful colored jewel, perhaps gold or yellow to protect your third chakra, a significant symbolic and literal location of immunity, your thymus gland. The thymus gland creates protective immune system biochemicals such as interleukin and interferon. You can wear protective jewelry, or a gold "QLink" for actual EMIT (electro-magnetic frequencies) protection from people, places, computers, and other electromagnetic equipment. You can use your powerful Subconscious Mind to extend the field around your car, your dwelling, and your place of work. Your positive force field actively repels negative energy and any kind of boundary violations. Have certainty that your vibrational force field is pro-tecting you from energy leaks both great and small.

TEACHING BY EXAMPLE

For most of us, maintaining the ability to say "No" in a positive way is a lifetime educational process. You will learn by doing, and you will also teach others by example. In living your own truth, you clarify who is responsible for what. If a friend asks for advice once or twice, you can willingly choose to give it. If he or she continues to ask for advice without having taken any actions to change the situation, you may experience an "energy leak," perhaps detrimental to your own well-being. You may decide to stop to giving advice at that point. In teaching by example, you improve your ability to connect directly with the *Quantum Hologram*, and you also show others how to ignite their own candles' source of light.

In this way, you and those around you are better able to build and sustain thoroughly positive vibra-tional energy. When staying up all night with a sick child, assisting an elderly parent, a friend, or stranger in crisis, you find the internal energy and strength. You may be exhausted in the moment, but you quickly recover and are a better person for your gift. Volunteering love and service in this way is the very opposite of energy leakage. As much as you give, you immediately feel restored. In these situations, we seem to resonate at higher levels than usual, in Flow, connecting with the *Quantum Hologram*. There's a profound sense of joy and "Oneness with all Creation."

WELCOMING RESISTANCE

Recognizing and embracing resistance is a key element of setting energetic boundaries. Begin by accepting the fact that inertia is natural.

Any complex system — whether it's our individual cells, our whole bodies, our minds, or our Spirit — is most comfortable remaining right where it is. A system is a combination of elements that work together to perform a specific function. The most important job of each and every part of any system is to preserve the integrity and life of the system itself. A cell is a complete and whole system, which is a part of larger systems (the digestive system, the circulatory system, the central nervous system), which in turn are part of the complete human or animal being. This being, whole and complete in itself, is also part of larger systems — a family, neighborhood, city, religion, Spiritual tradition, personal philosophy, county, state, nation, and even the Milky Way galaxy!

Complex interactions between systems both create and reflect the precision and symmetry of the functioning of all systems. In addition, all systems, from the minute to the celestial, are in constant *Resonance* with the *Realm of the Miraculous*, instantaneously sending, receiving, and performing the functions embodied in the ever-present energetic message that *We Are All One.*

Within that context, we human beings resist change, at least initially. We are creatures of habit. Our tried and true ways of doing things often go unquestioned and unexamined. We often operate as though change is certainly inconvenient, possibly dangerous, and potentially disastrous. Our habits have developed over years, and they may be subconsciously linked to survival, although there may be no real adaptive connection between our habitual ways of doing things and our actual well-being. We may be in the habit of eating our evening meal at six, and defend that habit as though it were of great importance, when, in fact, we could dine at five or seven with no negative consequences.

Because we are so embedded in habits, for many of us, the cultivation of flexibility and openness to change has to become a conscious practice, to clear the way for us to recognize the synchronicities that the Universe orchestrates all around us, many times a day. In order to achieve all of *Our Heart's Most Treasured Desires*, we must bring to conscious awareness our own internal resistance to change. As we become more aware of our own habit patterns, we strive to cultivate compassion and empathy for ourselves when we drift back into our old ways.

Greet your awareness of slipping back as positive information that allows you to do something different.

WHEN OTHERS RESIST YOUR CHANGE

When you change, those around you are forced to change, whether they want to or not. When one part of a system changes vibration, all other parts of the system reverberate. Each decision you may make carries with it a set of consequences. If you want to quit your job and live your dream, for instance, your spouse, your family, and your friends must respond and react. When you initiate change, you will find that the system impacted by the change you want will more than likely respond by trying to restore the old equilibrium of comfort and predictability. And the reality is, the initial response of the impacted system is usually an intense attempt to restore "the way things used to be."

If you ask your teenager for a room "cleanup," you may hear that, "Nobody else's parents make them do this stupid stuff," or, "None of my friends like you," or, "I'm not doing that, no matter how much you threaten me," or even, "I hate you." So be sure to translate "I hate you" into the truth, which the teenager just isn't mature enough to articulate. If he or she had the appropriate life experience and maturity, he or she would say, "I love you because you care enough about me to set appropriate limits and take the risk that I won't like you or love you." In the same way, you can understand others' angry, sullen, uncooperative responses, even their attempts to undermine the positive changes you are making for yourself and those around you, for what they really are: an attempt to restore the previous balance of the system. Remain tenacious! After all, you haven't made change capriciously, or without careful thought. Recognize others' attempts to resist change as fear-based, automatic, inertial reflexes. Perceive the negative responses as a sign that your plan is working. Transform the boos and hisses into resounding applause.

ENERGETIC MARTIAL ARTS

Practicing "energetic martial arts" will defuse any negative energy directed toward you. Remember: negative responses are directed toward you because you are changing in positive ways that will, in fact, help all those in your energetic field. Don't expect those around you to understand this. They are invested in preserving the status quo so that their predictable worlds can remain just that.

You can actively practice energetic martial arts by predicting that others are going to have negative responses to your change. Predicting negative responses helps you understand what is happening and provides you with strength in Body, Mind, and Spirit. In the everyday world, this means creating positive structures that support your goals. You invite others to discuss their responses to your changes, and you listen with attention. You place a limit on how long the discussion can go on — 10 minutes to half an hour. You let others know that you will not discuss the change outside of appointed times, and if they try to break this reasonable boundary, you will simply leave the room.

You envision, perhaps morning, noon, and night, that the change has already taken place. You luxuriate in your feeling-based knowing that the change is already complete. In this process, you assist yourself and others to be more whole and complete. You connect with the *Quantum Hologram* of Divine Intelligence, the source for strength and commitment to successful completion of your Experiment.

ENERGETIC ACCOUNTABILITY

Katie had grown up in a family where there was never enough. Never enough nurturing, never enough money, never enough fun, never enough joy. Katie was in her mid-forties, married, with three teenage boys. Her husband had treated Katie as if she was never enough, every single day of their 25 years of marriage.

Throughout her marriage, Katie had always worked outside the home, first as a receptionist/secretary for a small real estate firm. Clients and agents absolutely loved Katie. She was efficient, a hard worker, and exquisitely sensitive to the needs of everyone around her. After three years, the company offered her an apprenticeship with their top agent and paid for her to go to real estate school. She passed the exam with flying colors. The office was so busy that she got the overflow clients. She was sharp and intelligent, and seemed to have a nose for finding great deals, making both buyers and sellers happy.

Katie still found the time to be lovingly involved with her sons — assisting with schoolwork, supporting their activities, and making special time for each of them. Once a month Katie rotated taking one of the boys out somewhere special. Each boy got to choose his favorite activity, as long as it was age appropriate and she could manage it financially.

Eight months before she came to see me, Katie's husband had left her for a younger woman. Katie was absolutely devastated by the vicious and sadistic behavior of her husband during the divorce process. He locked her out of the house, refused to pay child support, and attempted to turn her children against her. Because she was such a good and consistent mother, Katie's boys weren't swayed by their father's attempted character assassination. Katie gave up her rightful share of the community assets, just to stop the abusive process created by her husband.

Katie came to me for assistance in healing herself: Body, Mind, and Spirit. She wanted to feel worthwhile, instead of feeling worthless. She also wanted to lose weight and create financial security for herself and her children. Katie sheepishly admitted to me that she had two secret desires that she had never told anyone. She had always wished that she could have millions of dollars and a body she felt proud in.

Sound Health, Sound Wealth

After our initial meeting, Katie and I worked together on the telephone, once a week for eight months. Our initial focus was on nutrition and pleasurable exercise. Katie lost 35 pounds, without dieting, in the first four months we worked together. She educated herself about appropriately chosen food as the sacred fuel for the temple of her body, and she learned to listen carefully to her body, tuning in to her real needs and wants, instead of using food habitually as a way to care for herself in the moment.

Our next task together was to enhance Katie's internal real self so that she would feel more worthy and deserving of good things in all areas of her life. Given the neglect and emotional impoverishment she had survived in childhood, Katie had herself created a remarkably strong foundation of good values, honesty, compassion, and empathy — hard to imagine given the way she had been treated most of her life. One of her most difficult adversaries was her own Internal Critic, incessantly accusing her ("You are a fat pig. You never do anything right.") and injecting her with toxic feelings of shame, disgust, and self-loathing. The assaults of her Internal Critic left Katie feeling exhausted, drained, and devastated.

One positive characteristic of the Internal Critic is its <u>internal</u> nature. When you are armed with effective interventions to turn down the volume, or completely turn off the vicious Internal Critic attacks, you are dealing with something inside you. Unlike freeway traffic, the weather, world conflicts, or other people, here, inside yourself, you can eventually, small step by small step, have absolute and complete control. I assisted Katie in choosing specific techniques to quiet the cruel words and feelings projected onto her by the Internal Critic. She learned to set impenetrable energetic boundaries so that she was no longer tortured by her own internal environment

Over time, we began to focus on dealing specifically with her husband. Katie got caller ID and refused to talk to her husband, or even listen to his messages, except when the children were with him. She insisted that any communication about the children be done by email, except for health emergencies. Her attorney helped her craft a reasonable interim visitation schedule.

I assisted Katie to be prepared when her husband raised the stakes in response to her setting appropriate energetic boundaries. I explained that when one person in a relationship changes, the other person responds by trying to restore the old balance in the system. I assisted Katie to understand that her husband's resistance to change was the evidence that she was in fact doing the right things. She became an expert in energetic martial arts.

Her husband was enraged that he couldn't continue his habitual abuse and began to stalk her. She got a restraining order, which he promptly broke. He was arrested and spent one night in jail. Fortunately that was the end of the stalking.

One day about seven months into our work together, I received a phone call from Katie, asking if she could meet with me immediately. Because she had to travel quite a distance to meet with me in person, I asked if anything was wrong. She replied, "No, I just want to see you." When Katie arrived for the appointment, her eyes were sparkling *and she absolutely vibrated health, joy, and well-being. She handed me a check. I remember it was printed on green safety paper. The check was made out to her in the amount of $8 million. This check was the result of a highly imaginative mini-mall deal that Katie had put together, benefiting the land seller, the buyers, and an eco-friendly small construction company. Sound Health and Sound Wealth indeed!*

Katie had corrected her own energetic leak and set firm energetic boundaries. She learned to welcome resistance as a sign of change, and learned how to practice energetic martial arts. She had used her real estate acumen to parlay small profits, to reinvest bigger, and to create an astounding profit physically, emotionally, Spiritually, and financially.

WELCOMING WEALTH WITHOUT SHAME OR GUILT

Katie's secret wish to have millions is a wish that many people have. We may at times felt awkward about our desire for financial abundance.

Sometimes, we associate financial success with greed and selfishness, because we have seen the misuse of power by those who take from the world and give back nothing. In addition, most of us have been around people with money who try to elevate themselves because they are rich, by putting others down. None of us want to be that kind of contemptuous elitist.

I believe that money is a significant form of Life Force. We ourselves are the decision makers who calibrate and assign specific frequencies for the ways in which Life Force in the form of money goes out into the world. You can free yourself from old beliefs that money equals greed and selfishness. You can have as much abundance as you need and desire, <u>and</u> be of love and service in the world. Money and altruism are not mutually exclusive.

Perhaps you have a vision of helping children, funding important research to cure cancer or AIDS, or maybe you want to protect endangered species, save the rain forest, or help fund the development of non-petroleum energy sources that will power automobiles efficiently and clean up the environment. Maybe you want to paint or sculpt or write. Maybe you want to have more time to spend with family, children, or friends. Maybe you want to hang out and have total freedom to live in the moment. There are enough resources for each one of us on this planet to have millions of dollars, without anyone else having to suffer. So teach by example. By your own experience of abundance, you can teach all of us that there is more than enough for each of us to enjoy true abundance.

NOBLE FRIENDS

Creating energetic boundaries and accessing the power of "No" is not always easy. Fortunately, these are not steps that we need to take entirely on our own. The very important category of people whom I call "Noble Friends" are here to help us — despite the fact that we may not even recognize them at first sight, or, perhaps, even for a very long time.

Noble Friends arrive in a variety of guises and disguises. Sometimes, and perhaps even for years, *noble* might be the last word we'd use to describe people we perceive as unsupportive, self-centered, aggressive, manipulative, and even dangerous. In some cases, we view Noble Friends as our enemies, and they may indeed act like enemies from whom we absolutely need to escape. Noble Friends are people whose behavior toward us, on the surface, has been significantly more negative than positive. For example, a fierce professional competitor who attempts to tarnish your reputation or character, whether overtly or even subtly, might be a Noble Friend.

Noble Friends teach us lessons we don't necessarily want to learn — truths about who truly loves and supports us, and who is in a relationship with us primarily to promote themselves at our expense. Literally, *noble* means, "of an exalted moral character." Noble Friends often do not fit that definition themselves. Instead, they provide <u>us</u> with the opportunity to further develop our own worth and worthiness. The nobility of your Noble Friends is in the nobility that they make available to you.

A Noble Friend may appear in the form of a parent, friend, family member, spouse, or even a stranger. They may have no desire to do harm. They may be confused, attempting to do the right thing. They may even have perfectly good intentions. However, their inability or unwillingness to interact smoothly with us is like a grain of sand in an oyster. It can culminate in a beautiful pearl, but for a long time the oyster would like nothing better than to get rid of it.

Sometimes Noble Friends deliberately camouflage themselves with purposeful intent to mislead us, consciously covering up who they really are and what they really want. On other occasions, they will intentionally act in ways that are difficult for us to cope with; they may even behave in ways that cause us significant pain. At a deeper level, however, Noble Friends always offer us the opportunity to choose the high road, to take the next steps in our own development toward inner and outer abundance. With time and reflection, we come to recognize how those who may have hurt us have also provided us with crucial opportunities for choice and growth.

Noble Friends give us priceless gifts, <u>sometimes gifts that we absolutely do not want to receive, often gifts that we want to ignore, delay opening, and perhaps avoid altogether. One of the gifts Noble Friends can give is in fact the subject of this chapter: They can give us the noble opportunity of saying "No."</u>

Consider this: There are many positive things we can do in the world. There are many things we can give, and many different ways we can contribute. But the best way for one person to give is very often not the best for others. It can take a long time to discover how you can have a positive impact on the world and the people around you. Sometimes it can take years. Sometimes it can take a lifetime. It's a discovery you need to make for yourself — but while you're on the path toward making the discovery, be careful of letting others tell you where you should be going. Also, it is often helpful to remember that being careful doesn't mean being hostile. People who don't have a perfect understanding of your needs and the essence of who you are are not necessarily your enemies. It's much better to think of them as your Noble Friends. <u>And what lessons they teach us</u>: compassion for self and others, patience, tolerance, forgiveness, acceptance, nonjudgment, detachment, and not accepting negative criticism.

Imagine a little girl who's very good at drawing, or who can run fast, or who has a talent for putting puzzles together. It can be almost anything, but there's a particular skill that this girl has and she enjoys using that skill. Then one day her parents decide she should take piano lessons. But it turns out, unfortunately, that she has very little aptitude for the piano. She doesn't really enjoy the externally imposed struggle to do something that she's not good at. She'd rather develop her real talent, whatever it might be, but now the time she can devote to that has been diminished, because she has to use that time practicing the piano.

A mistake is being made here. Playing the piano is a wonderful thing, but it's not wonderful when it takes someone away from doing other things that are also wonderful. Of course, it might be argued that playing the piano is more wonderful than putting together puzzles or running fast — because the piano represents culture, and it has associations with Beethoven and Mozart, and people get all dressed up to hear piano recitals in huge concert halls. All that is true, but even standing on your head is much more important than playing the piano or the violin if you really find joy in it — and perhaps there's a way that it will bring joy to other people as well.

On occasion, a Noble Friend may ask you to give of your time, or you may be asked to make a financial contribution to a particular organization, or you may be asked to do something else that, in and of itself, might be quite worthy and wonderful. But for you it might be the equivalent of playing the piano in the example just cited. It may not be the best way for <u>you</u> to contribute at this particular time in <u>your</u> life. It may not be the best thing you can do toward creating joy and fulfillment, both for yourself and for other people. When that's the case, the best thing is simply to say "No."

It's so important to understand and assert yourself in this way. You need to be able to say, "I realize that working in a hospital is a great thing, but it's really not the best contribution I can make at this time. For me, it's better to draw," or to teach drawing, or to do whatever "your thing" really is.

CONNECTING TO THE POWER OF 'NO'

Find a comfortable place in which to sit and write. Make sure you have privacy and will not be interrupted.

Think of some situations in your life when you would like to say "No!" but you don't. Create separate lists of these situations in relation to your Body, Mind, and Spirit. Be excruciatingly honest. You can often identify problematic patterns of thinking, feeling, and acting by being a careful observer of yourself. Notice the feelings you have in situations in which you feel you can't say "No!" to others, as well as to yourself — and notice how the feelings recirculate in your thoughts. When we don't say "No!" when we need to or want to, we often feel uncomfortable, resentful, angry, irritated, anxious, and perhaps, even somewhat embarrassed or depressed.

The following examples of saying "Yes" to yourself and others, when you really want to say "No!" may help you clarify the areas that most need your attention. In order to say "No" and have it work effectively, you first need to identify the specific problem. Next, Make a Decision about the outcome you want. You will then discover the ingredients of the solution. Give yourself a reasonable time frame in which to change. Be prepared to use energetic martial arts to triumph over internal and external resistance. Rehearsing your "No's" and using unflagging persistence play starring roles in your success.

Joe's First Thoughts: "I know I need to exercise. I'm 25 pounds overweight, and my doctor has told me my cholesterol ratios are not great. Between work and the kids' activities and getting done what has to be done, I just don't exercise. When I get home at night, I just want to kick back and relax. I think I deserve to rest after working so hard."

First Feelings: Self-righteous, worried, concerned, anxious, guilty, irritated, frustrated, angry, helpless, confused, disappointed.

Second Thoughts: "If I am completely honest, it's clear that the source of the problem is me. Since that's the truth of it, I know I can fix this problem. Basically, I create the no-exercise problem because I come up with some pretty good excuses about why it's okay for me to eat a lot of whatever I want, and not exercise. I guess I think I deserve to laze around because I work so hard."

Making a Decision About the Outcome-Action Plan:
"The outcome I want is to be able to do some kind of regular exercise that isn't huffing and puffing at the gym. For me to stick with exercise, it'll have to be something I like, or at least something I don't hate."

Creating the Solution with a Reasonable Timetable:
"Within the next two weeks I will get schedules for all the softball and basketball teams, choose one, and start to participate."

Using Energetic Martial Arts to Defeat Internal and External Resistance: "I've signed up for the Boomer softball team. They meet three times a week. If it's snowing or raining, we go to the gym next door and shoot hoops. I don't get any beer or chips unless I make the game or practice. I'm getting excited about this.

"I have been able to do a great job of sticking with my rewarded exercise program. I've been doing this for the last four months and I've dropped 15 pounds without even trying. I saw my doctor three weeks ago. My cholesterol ratios are going in the right direction. My wife seems pretty impressed by the whole deal, and we're having more fun together. I guess I feel better about myself all the way around."

Darlene's First Thoughts: "I know I need to stop listening to my mother complaining all the time. She blames my dad for everything, and she blames me too, in a way. She always talks about dropping out of college to get married and have children and how glamorous her life would have been if she'd pursued a career. Of course, now it's too late, so I kind of feel blamed for that, too."

First Feelings: Frustrated, resentful, angry, helpless, hurt, invisible, sad, confused.

Second Thoughts: "At first I thought the whole problem was my mother. After talking with two friends, I can see that my mom's been the way she is forever. Now that I'm out on my own, I don't have to put up with her nonstop complaining and blaming anymore. I know I am allowing this problem to go on, because I just listen and don't say anything to stop her. The hardest part of this is that she is my mother. I can be really assertive with people at work because I feel accepted by them. I know they like and respect me. I have this thing about being a good daughter and never making my mother mad or upset."

Making a Decision About the Outcome-Action Plan: "I decided that what I wanted was not to have to listen more than 20 minutes a week, in the beginning, to my mom's complaining. Then I'll cut the complaining time down five minutes a month. That way, it will take only four months to get to the no-complaining goal."

Creating the Solution with a Reasonable Timetable: "I decided to see a psychologist to help me with this — it seemed pretty big to me. Dr. Reynolds was great. She was easy to talk with and very results oriented. It took only eight sessions to figure out the action plan and get my self-confidence boosted high enough to tackle this. As it turned out, my mother seemed like the hardest person in the world to be myself with."

Using Energetic Martial Arts to Defeat Internal and External Resistance: "I knew my mother would go to any lengths to keep our relationship just the way it was. I rehearsed my lines over and over, and I was prepared to actually hang up the phone if she started in. Of course, I told her all this when I took her to lunch. I told her that I loved her and that I want us to have the best relationship we can. I told her that her complaining and blaming me for her missed opportunities made me feel terrible and that I just wasn't going to live that way anymore. It was needless suffering, because all my silent listening never made her feel better. If it had, she would have stopped her negative behavior.

"She cried, she got mad, she pouted, she threatened, she got sick, or at least she said she did. All because I gently cut her negative phone calls down to 10 minutes twice a week. Oh — I did tell her that if she wanted more time with me, it would have to be doing fun activities together, or talking about the good things that are going on for both of us. I was determined to get this big mess out of my wonderful life, and guess what, I did. I had to wait her out, and keep restating my boundaries, but my mom has changed her behavior and our relationship is definitely better."

I know you can implement the appropriate "No's" you need and want in your life so that you can experience less unnecessary stress and suffering and more effortless ease, as you live, each and every moment, more and more in the world of *Your Heart's Most Treasured Desires.*

Chapter Five

The Principle of Transforming Time

The ability to solve time problems offers us the freedom to expand, contract, and transcend time. Transcending our limiting beliefs about time is crucial for healing ourselves, our relationships, and our planet. When we solve time problems, we are really resolving our current perceptions about time. We are challenging the age-old myths that our world is, and must be, a world of lack and limitation, filled with things that we will run out of — like time!

How many times in your life have you been a hundred percent present while reading a book, enjoying an enchanting conversation, holding your child or grandchild, writing, painting, hiking with your dog, listening to or playing music, and, glancing at your watch, you realize that hours have actually gone by — hours that seemed like minutes? These miraculous events often feel like *Holy Moments*. In these magical moments, you have transcended the culturally defined artificial, linear, and perceptual construct of time.

When you *Make a Decision* and intend to change your relationship with time, it is increasingly possible to string transcendent moments together like a beautiful and exotic strand of pearls.

Three years ago, I was driving up a spectacular two-lane mountain road, on my way to Lake Tahoe. It was about eight in the morning and I noticed three bicyclists toiling up the 45-degree road. There was a very narrow bike lane, and, although the cyclists were wearing helmets and appropriate gear, I remember feeling concerned about their safety. The road required my undivided attention, as there were nonstop hairpin turns and the drop-off was, at points, thousands of feet down.

I stopped to buy gas and some bottled water about a quarter of the way up the mountain. As I looked around at the emerald-green meadows dotted with purple and orange wildflowers, the deep blue-green ancient pines, and the cerulean sky that stretched on for miles, I felt absolutely blessed to be alive this day, this moment.

About three-quarters of the way to the top, I saw that the three bikers were stopped at a pull-off, waving me down. I braked and stopped. I had guessed the group to be in their mid-thirties. As a tall man walked over to me, I noticed that although his body was tight and lean, his face looked a bit older than I had thought. He told me he had hit a rock that had bent his tire frame and asked for a ride to the top of the mountain. As we stowed the bikes on top of my car, Walt introduced his wife Ginny and their daughter

Margo. As we drove, the family told me that they had begun cycling together five years ago, after their yearly health checkups revealed unhealthy weight gains for all three of them. They had previously enjoyed good health and were determined to do whatever it would take to create and enjoy great health.

They did some reading and consulted a Naturopathic Medical Doctor. Based on her recommendations and their own ongoing research, they picked a kind of physical exercise they all liked — cycling — switched to organically grown food, and took a variety of individualized "food grown" nutritional supplements. They also drank oxygenated alkalized water. Ginny and Margo told me that they also worked with a dermatologist, to improve their skin without any cosmetic surgery. Walt admitted that he had initially resisted the "girlie" products the women used, but their results were so incredible that he couldn't hold out for long. I guessed their ages and was wrong by decades. Walt and Ginny were in their mid-seventies and looked to be in their mid-fifties. Margo was 55 and looked 40.

The Duncans had put their health as their top priority, consulted experts and educated themselves, picked an exercise they enjoyed, and created their own support group to sustain the sometimes difficult discipline of regular exercise. They rejected the idea that aging is inevitable. They also told me that they believed the aging process was actually <u>reversible</u>.

One needn't be a mystic, a holy person, or a quantum physicist to alter the collective space-time agreement. In fact, you already do this — when you dream, meditate, relax deeply, or experience synchronistic moments. These are authentic moments of timelessness.

TRANSFORMING TIME

The year was 1922, and the location was Paris, France. Although it didn't make headlines around the world, a very unique public debate took place on a subject that affects all of us, but that few of us ever really sit down and talk about. The subject was <u>time</u>. But the topic of the debate was not the only thing that made it unique. One of the participants was the French philosopher Henri Bergson, whose principal areas of investigation were (interestingly enough) time, memory, and laughter. His opponent was Albert Einstein, who, as the saying goes, "needs no introduction."

Without going into details of the fairly challenging content of this discussion, it did produce some enlightening and surpassingly practical insights. Einstein disagreed with Bergson's interpretation of time in his concept of relativity. According to Einstein's theory, basic elements of the Universe such as space, mass, speed, and time are all interdependent, or "relative." The flow of time in a particular environment, therefore, will vary according to the speed with which that environment is traveling through space. The faster we go, the slower time proceeds — and if we were to go fast enough, time would theoretically stop altogether. We do not, however, experience changes in the rate of time when we fly in a plane or even ride in a car — first, because the change is almost infinitely small, and second, because we are not constituted to think of time (or anything else, for that matter) as they "really are" in terms of theoretical physics.

When Einstein said, "Time and space are modes by which we think and are not conditions in which we live," he did not mean that time and space exist only in our thoughts. On the contrary, he meant that our thoughts of time and space — that is, our everyday consciousness — do not express the realities of time and space as they exist on the scale of the Universe as a whole. We are "wrong" if we think time happens at the same rate when we're sitting in a chair as when we're in a jet plane. We are often unaware of the scientific information about time that could have significant impact on how we understand and make use of time, in ways that would enhance us and our world.

Bergson looked at time differently. For him, there were really two categories of time, neither of which was more real or more important than the other. On one hand, there was time in the sense that Einstein described it: time as an element of the physical laws of the Universe, as a component of the "space-time" that is the fabric of all reality. But there was also a form of time that Bergson called "perceived duration" — that is, time experienced as a function of our consciousness. The revolution in physical science that occurred in the early years of the 20th century erased the distinction between subjective experience and objective reality. Bergson specifically extended this to include time, or at least one of the two kinds of time that he envisioned.

For practical purposes, the areas of agreement between the two debaters are more significant than the points on which they disagreed. Both Bergson and Einstein acknowledged that time is something that we perceive and experience in our consciousness. They disagreed about the significance of "consciousness time" in the physical laws of the Universe, but neither denied its existence.

Let's look more closely at what this means. A strong cosmological argument can be made, for example, that time is not something that is happening but is in fact something that has already happened. It may be that we live in an instantaneous Universe that is "decoded" by our consciousness as a gradual progression through time. "Time," according to the physicist John Wheeler, "'is something we've created in order to prevent everything from happening at once." Wheeler's statement brings us back to the idea that time is not an absolute value. It's a variable, like speed and mass. And it also varies with our consciousness. The meaning of time, and even the <u>existence</u> of time, can't be separated from how we experience it.

Many people have experiences that would seem to support this. In emergencies such as explosions or auto accidents, time really does seem to slow down and elongate to an amazing degree. An event that takes only a few seconds on a stop watch can seem much, much longer from the participant's point of view. Whether it's "really" much longer is where Henri Bergson and Albert Einstein disagree — but there's no doubt that time seemed to slow down in the consciousness of the individual.

There are other examples of time slowing down, sometimes as a result of human intention. Physiologically, for instance, it's impossible for a professional baseball player to react quickly enough to a well-thrown fast ball in order to get a hit. There simply isn't enough time for a human body to process the incoming information about the flight of the ball and to swing the bat accordingly. Yet the fact remains: Players do hit fast balls. It happens all the time. Furthermore, many players have developed an ability to actually slow down the flight of the ball as they perceive it. They can intentionally access the elongation of time that takes place involuntarily during car accidents. From their point of view, a fast ball takes a much longer time to cross home plate than it would for you or me. Once again, we might ask whether it "really" takes a longer time — and once again the answer depends on which authority you consult. But one thing is certain: Some people can hit fast balls a lot better than others, and part of the reason is their ability to control their experience of time. By creating a vibration of intention, they can cause time to resonate. Just as the strings of a guitar, amplified by the body of the instrument, can play the note that a musician intends, there are people who can "play" time like a well-loved familiar melody. And one of those people can be you.

THE TIME IS NOW

Your life includes approximately 30,000 days. How do you want to experience them? Will they rush past like cars on a freeway, or will they proceed in a perfectly paced order like the notes of a symphony?

What do you wish to accomplish and experience? Who and what do you love? Do you have time for your most cherished family, friends, nature, organizations, personal interests, exercise, recreation, and relaxation? Do you have time for yourself, to use in any way that you desire? Do you ever have time to just "be"?

You really do have the power to create a new relationship with time — a connection that is exciting, magical, and wondrous. Time will be your ally, rather than your antagonist. Your "deadlines" will become "lifelines." Your "to do" list will become a "have done" list. Without ever consciously choosing to do so, you have most likely lived your life as though time were an inviolable reality. Yet, as Henri Bergson suggested in that debate many years ago, we define time by our beliefs and experience of it, not by the reality of time itself. When we change our beliefs about time, we can change our experience of it — and in a very real sense, we can change time itself.

Several years ago I consulted with a couple who were absolutely ready to embrace new concepts about time, and how to make it work in their favor.

Kristen and Tom were in their early forties. Kristen was great with people, and had worked for years as a production manager in the garment industry. Tom was more introverted, with decades of experience as a mechanical engineer in a company that manufactured office equipment. Tom and Kristen were ready to use the strengths and discard the weaknesses of the traditional models of business building. They shared a dream of creating a small business manufacturing colorful, innovative organic fiber children's clothing.

They understood how to make time work for them in both magical and scientific ways. They quickly mastered the tools of compressing, expanding, and transcending time, transforming the laborious SBA loan paperwork "deadline" into a "lifeline." Through their use of Future Memories, *Tom and Kristen got on the fast track: Their loan was fully funded in six months. By* Making a Decision, *they created a company that would operate like a small village. Employees received competitive wages and were additionally compensated with a share of company stock every six months, providing a compelling "buy in" that accelerated the company's success. High-quality onsite childcare was available at reasonable cost, and employees received five compensated hours a week to* spend in the small but comfortable gym/meditation/yoga center on premises.

Kristen and Tom were mindful about their choice of the workplace: They knew that the specific quality of the environment was crucial to productivity and employee satisfaction. The old brick building they selected was beautiful, framed by fruit trees and sturdy perennial plants and flowers. They did a low-cost, quick makeover: lots of natural light, comfortable workspaces, elegant use of color, verdant live plants, the rhythmic sounds of indoor waterfalls. Their managerial style was "relationships, relationships, relationships." Every employee, vendor, and customer felt valued, because, in fact, they <u>were</u> valued for their particular unique contributions.

Time for exercise and relaxation were built into the work culture, thereby eliminating another significant block of time that employees would have had to spend commuting to a gym or yoga class. Tom and Kristen worked smart. They knew that concern about the quality of childcare often contributes to tardiness and missed work, and that employees who exercise regularly have significantly stronger immune response, more optimism, higher productivity, and fewer missed days of work.

Every evening, Kristen and Tom relived and relished the accomplishments of the day. The problem-solving glitches had been relegated to their meeting in the last hour before they left work. Every morning, they connected together in a five-minute meditation, sometimes in silence, sometimes talking.

By the third quarter of their first year, net profits boldly outstripped costs. A year and a half after the official opening *day, a private investor made a substantial offer to buy the business; however, Kristen and Tom did not want to sell it. Eric, the private investor, was so excited by Tom and Kristen's creation of a "human friendly" work environment that he was willing to modify his offer from buying the business outright to going into a partnership with Tom and Kristen. After long heartfelt discussion and deep soul searching, Kristen and Tom decided to accept, structuring the deal to use the influx of cash to begin franchising their store. Eric headed up the one-person new division devoted to making the franchise concept operational. Three years later, the franchise division brought in five times the net profit margin of the manufacturing part of the operation.*

It was a pleasure and a joy to work with Kristen and Tom — their willingness to "ride the wave" of new ideas about time and success was remarkable, and paid off for them in all ways, Body, Mind, and Spirit.

TIME POVERTY

Two hundred years ago, the Industrial Era was supposed to usher in more free time to individuals. Yet, the pendulum swung entirely the other way. Life got busier, not easier. Many businesses, restaurants, and stores expanded their days and hours of operation. Some operate 24 hours a day, and the Internet is always open. Rather than offering us more freedom and time, industry and technology have done the opposite. Objects and experiences once available as luxuries for the privileged few have become "must haves" for many of us. We work more to acquire more, but we often don't have the time to use our toys.

Many of us are suffering from what I call "time poverty." The idea of having an abundance of time to rest, restore, rejuvenate, contemplate, and recreate does not exist for many people. Some amount of unrest in our world is created by the dream that "having it all" leads to happiness and life satisfaction. Ongoing research has demonstrated that "having it all" often leads to frustration, because there is no time to enjoy the "all," and there always seems to be more "all" to obtain. Time poverty often results in impoverished and impulsive decision making — individually and collectively — making our personal and global existence worse, not better.

In attempting to "feel better" and experience an immediate "state change," away from anxiety, fear, fatigue, emotional stress, or pain, we may make unwise choices in the moment. In stressful situations, we are much more vulnerable, and much more likely to use "quick fixes" in the form of alcohol, smoking, drugs, shopping, eating, or hundreds of other distractions.

In addition, when we are faced with high-intensity stressful events or with the cumulative effects of chronically stressful events, our brains just don't work as well as usual. Our difficulties in successfully managing stress and reinstating internal equilibrium inevitably create depleting brain changes. No matter how intelligent or experienced, we are all, each and every one of us, vulnerable to high-intensity stressful situations or to the chronic depleting effects of a series of stressful occurrences.

Problem solving and making decisions from states of anxiety, fatigue, stress, and fear yield far different results than problem solving from a relaxed, intuitive, centered, and balanced state of being. Stress and anxiety access different biochemistry in the brain and a different *Resonance* in your heart than do states of relaxation, balance, peace, and satisfaction. Essentially, different neurochemicals create different outcomes.

Even if you aren't personally experiencing the tremendous crush of time problems, you may be reverberating to the electromagnetic frequencies of the fear and frustration of those directly around you or those in the "collective morphogenetic fields."

In addition to time poverty, another source of major unrest in the world results from people not having their basic needs met — essential needs for enough food, clean water, shelter, and adequate medical care. Across the globe, many of us are diverted away from the real problems that plague most countries (hunger, inadequate or nonexistent medical care, lack of clean water, extreme poverty, deforestation, lack of real political choices) by the lure of the merchandised "quick fix": the cool shoes, bling jackets, jewelry, travel, and toys — the things that are proffered to fill the holes of emptiness, loneliness, helplessness, anxiety, depression, confusion, sadness, and anger in our emotionally, Spiritually, and sometimes even physically impoverished individual selves. The marketed quick fix is endemic to collective consciousness and is, therefore, nearly invisible. We have allowed ourselves to be persuaded that if only we wear this brand, or drive that brand, or have the other brand, then we are okay, and our world is okay.

Rich abundance in all forms is to be encouraged and supported, but never as a substitution for reality or at punishing costs to others.

Electromagnetic frequencies of anger, fear, and frustration, in collective consciousness, are increasingly known and felt by most of us — amplified by the increasing gap between what is "sold" as reality (everything is really fine, the terrorists are them, not us) and what is, in fact, the unretouched reality, transmitted in shocking detail by instantaneous media coverage. What may have been subconscious, not known, by many, is more and more quickly becoming known to nearly all, rising to consciousness. The same instant media that pitch certain brands of athletic shoes as the solution to the emptiness inside a living human being also show us the truth of lives impacted by war, famine, and natural disasters.

The anger, fear, anxiety, depression, hopelessness, helplessness, and outrage you feel when you see avoidable human suffering can serve as a critical catalyst to move you into changing what you can — even if it sometimes seems hopeless. A positive action plan to help yourself, help others, and help the world usually starts small for most of us. One phone call, one short letter, makes a difference. "One small step for each man and woman: a giant step for all humankind."

Transcending Time for Sound Health

In a "medicineless hospital" in Beijing, China, a woman suffering from a life-threatening cancerous tumor of the bladder was completely healed, within "real time" moments. The entire procedure was "live on video." Three healing practitioners placed themselves at the foot and on both sides of her bed.

The practitioners, using their voices and the power of compassionate healing intention, altered and transcended linear time and space to effect this healing. They each used a different sound mantra that held a universal healing significance for each of them. In two minutes and 40 seconds, witnesses observed the patient as her body became completely free of cancer. They literally watched the tumor lighten from a nearly black mass until it was absolutely colorless. In front of their eyes, the tumor began to shrink and completely disappeared. The practitioners bowed, clapped their hands once, and gave thanks for their ability to assist in the woman's complete recovery.

The integral consciousness-based approach to natural healing, the practice of medicine, and the transformation of the world is well under way. There is a collective planetary desire for healing through the transcendence of time, fueled by the increasing frequency of disturbing world events, informing us that we must move quickly to heal and save ourselves, all others, and our planet.

Painful, costly, and often lethal treatments for cancer and other diseases are being augmented or replaced by noninvasive transformative therapies that are truly mystical, magical, and scientific. Like a gentle and healing rain from the heavens, a new and beautiful emerald lake of consciousness is effervescing. This "jewel-like consciousness" is bringing to life the wisdom of the ages, buried for centuries, and is being substantiated with brilliant new paradigms in medicine and science. The focus of this integral consciousness is to transcend time by healing our separation from our true Source, our true selves, each other, Nature, and the world we collectively share.

By choosing to embrace our scientifically magical connectedness, we may literally solve the dangerous frightening limited linear perception of the inevitable doom and destruction of ourselves, each other, and Mother Earth. We begin this process by recognizing that we are each individual aspects of a greater whole. We are each like a particle of light in the *Quantum Hologram*: Each particle contains an entire blueprint of the whole. When we understand fully that We Are All One, we know that to harm another person, or being, in any way, is to harm ourselves.

Any philosophy, religion, or technology can be utilized to enrich and further All, or it can be used to elevate some and denigrate others. In each and every moment, we can choose either the healing wisdom of the Ancients or the diabolical wisdom of some sects of the Ancients. We can choose the Quantum Science frontier of healing or the Quantum Science frontier embodying weapons of mass destruction. <u>In each decision we make, we can ask ourselves, "Will this thought, action, or deed create more peace in my life, in the lives of others, and in the world?" or, "Will this thought, feeling, or action create more pain in my life, in the lives of others, and in the world?"</u>

We must be scrupulously honest and acknowledge that if we choose not to act, waiting passively for others to decide our destiny and the fate of our world, we give away our power to enhance the good, and still bear the responsibility that our refusal to act has profound effects on the outcome of every situation. Each intention we have and each behavior we engage in is essentially a vote for or against peace and well-being for ourselves and the world as a whole

The late Elizabeth Targ, a medical doctor and researcher at Stanford University, was one of the first to scientifically study the efficacy of compassionate nonlocal healing. Using double-blind studies, Dr. Targ transformed formerly esoteric ideas into a scientific model to demonstrate the quantum interrelatedness of those being studied. Her work exemplified the "Oneness" that we share with one another and with all life. Her work demonstrated the unifying principles that underlie the Body-Mind-Spirit connection.

Through *Compassionate Intention*, one can actually alter the physiology of another person instantly, faster than the speed of light, even if that person is on the other side of the world. An example of this principle is the "Love Study." The "sender" who is trained in *Compassionate Intention* is paired with a person in need who will be the "receiver" of loving and healing energy. The pair may exchange a sacred object that has significant meaning for both the sender and the receiver. The purpose of this exchange is to help both participants become more deeply focused.

Initial studies used a randomized double-blind protocol in which light was used to stimulate the visual cortex area of the brain of the sender after he or she reached an agreed-upon depth of meditative state. The sender then intentionally transmitted loving, healing, and compassionate thoughts to the receiver, who was often in pain or very ill. The sender and receiver were each in psychophysiology laboratories in separate locations, often as far away from one another as the United States and Australia.

Referred to as "Evoked Potential Research," the laboratory measurements that are used to demonstrate the quantum interconnectedness of the individuals studied include skin conductivity, heart rate, EEGs (electroencephalograms), and "real time," functional MRIs (magnetic resonance imaging).

These scientific healing studies and protocols demonstrate beyond the shadow of a doubt that we actually, measurably, transcend the linear fixed agreements about time. This research absolutely proves that the high *Resonance* of love and compassion resonates in the seen and the unseen, the atomic and the subatomic worlds.

In addition, research has demonstrated that the same profound healing may be accomplished through prayer. To be effective in prayer, one must learn to transmit a coherent signal through the field of Divine Intelligence in order to be of significant assistance to others. One could easily argue that these desired well-documented results must be in alignment with Karma or God's will, or they could not possibly occur.

Often the question arises as to whether one could also do harm, such as "murder at a distance," through the use of these same modalities of long-distance treatments directed toward others. I once had the opportunity to discuss these ideas with some former KGB agents. They admitted to me that after governmental changes in the early 1990s, they had been secretly publishing a New Age magazine for healing. They told me that, although they themselves had been engineers, they knew of others who had been specifically trained to cause heart attacks in enemies, using techniques of nonlocality.

In regard to the dark use of nonlocality, I also spoke with a medical doctor who had practiced for years in the Caribbean. He told me he had seen hundreds of incidents of Voodoo, in which the patient had received a "hex" from an individual or group, and later died. In almost all of the deaths that he had observed, the patient who had received the hex knew about it, was terrified and superstitious, and died, in spite of having no specific untoward clinical findings. The physician said that he believed that the power of the Subconscious Mind, mobilized through fear, made these deaths a self-fulfilling prophecy. <u>Anyone undergoing trauma of this nature may ward off the horrific negative strategies of others through the use of prayer and asking concerned others for support and *Compassionate Intention*</u>. Trained experts can assist those who are targeted negatively in a variety of ways, including the creation of energetic boundaries, which can be monitored through the use of sophisticated biofeedback modalities.

I have discussed these issues extensively with other authors who are on a variety of Spiritual paths. We all came to the same conclusion: Although malevolent and evil practices have existed in ancient times, as well as more currently in cults and many of our modern governments, ultimately, the high *Resonance* of love and compassion have a greater absolute power than does the low *Resonance* of judgment, fear, and hate.

To me, the answer is simply this: The higher consciousness states of love, compassion, and forgiveness have a much higher resonant effect in the limitless field of potentiality than do the lower consciousness states of war, anger, fear, and hate. This has been Spiritual truth through the ages, and now is established scientific fact. The damaging belief states and actions motivated by fear and hate are engaged in only by those who feel separate from any internal compassionate and empathic "real self," separate from others, and separate from our Divine Source.

THE POWER OF ONE

David Hawkins, M.D., Ph.D., author and psychiatrist, has proposed that <u>one person who resonates the high frequency vibrations of compassion, love, and forgiveness into the *Quantum Hologram* counterbalances 90,000 others who resonate the low frequency vibrations of fear, anger, rage, and hate.</u> Personally, I believe that the healing Consciousness, expressed through Right Action, of Jesus, Paramahansa Yogananda, Mother Teresa, Buddha, Confucius, Mahatma Gandhi, Martin Luther King Jr., and countless others has changed, and continues to change, our consciousness on this Earth. It takes enormous courage to engage in acts that proclaim, *"We Are All One."* For each of us, finding the will to act as if *We Are All One*, in ways great and mostly small, is how we heal ourselves and our world.

Behaving with empathy, courage, kindness, and dignity toward others, often facing seductive and sometimes coercive group pressure to comply with cruel, damaging behavior to others — taking the high road, no matter how small the stage — is our way to peace. The overarching belief that *We Are All One* lingers in the morphogenetic fields of consciousness and can be reliably accessed by heartfelt, Compassionate Intention.

Through this same focus and intention we may also assist the healing of our loved ones, and even strangers, sometimes immediately and dramatically. By doing so, we transcend our former limited and limiting perceptual agreements about time.

I take heart in the enormous increase in the general population's interest and participation in the pursuit of peace, health, and well-being for all that I am grateful to have observed over the past 30 years. I don't doubt that we have a long way to go in a very short time. However, I have tremendous hope, because many more people seem willing to share their experience, strength, and hope, given their concerns about the deteriorating state of our planet, when they, by nature, would prefer to live quiet and private lives. I am also very heartened by the work of many others.

By *Making a Decision* to do so, you can and will bring into your life those who wish to transcend time for healing, peace, and prosperity. You create your own internal *Resonance* of your desired support system, by anticipating doors magically opening, through synchronistic events. To stay in *Resonance* with your desires, it is often helpful to turn off the news and listen to informative, enjoyable audio programs, read books, and attend groups of those sharing your desire to transcend linear thinking and time problems. Staying in *Resonance* with your desires will provide bountiful overflowing rewards in all areas of your life, Body, Mind, and Spirit.

TAKING CONTROL OF TIME

<u>Time is within your control</u>. This is literally the truth — and it's a dramatic point of convergence between ancient teachings and modern insights. When you recognize that truth and act on it, you can change time from a tidal wave that threatens to engulf you, to a powerful force working for you in every moment.

The first step is discovering what you're doing with your time right now. And please note: <u>I said what you're doing with your time, not what your time is doing with you</u>. You are in control. Accept that responsibility, and seize that opportunity. How? It's really very simple. Just start keeping a record of how you actually spend your time.

A time log is a detailed, minute-by-minute diary of the day. It's a written record that lets you evaluate your activities and the time they required so that you can decide where changes need to be made. Keeping an accurate time log of all your activities lets you see with dazzling clarity exactly how much time you use, and how much you waste. It gives you the facts you need for making radical improvements in managing your time. And it brings the benefits that always come from writing things down and facing reality on the page in front of you.

To get maximum results from a time log, consider making a commitment to yourself to keep it for at least one full week. Seeing how you actually spend your time will definitely reveal many surprises — provided, of course, that you're absolutely honest in what you write down. It's no exaggeration to say that a time log is the single most important tactic for putting yourself in control of time.

Here's how to keep a time log. You may wish to start with a new notebook — one you'll be using exclusively for this purpose. Write the date at the top of each page, and then list six intentions that you want to fulfill during that day. Three of them should be oriented toward the material world — things you need to do in your work or to improve your physical health. These goals can include a letter you need to write, an article you want to read, a talk you want to have with a colleague, or time you want to set aside for exercise. The remaining three intentions should be Spiritually oriented. These can also involve physical actions, such as walking in nature or even gazing up at the clouds in the sky. Or they can focus on inner activities like mediation or prayer. They may require very little time, or perhaps quite a bit. The important thing is to build some focus on Spiritual growth into your goals for every day.

Once you've written your six intentions, note down the times you used to accomplish them during the day. And keep a record also of your other activities as the day goes on, including when you start and when you stop. This is a great way to identify the areas in which you were actively in control of your time, as well as those periods when time was just "happening" while you passively watched.

At the end of each day, look over what you've written. Were you able to accomplish your six intentions? If not, carry them over to the next day — and if you <u>did</u> accomplish your intentions, create six new ones. Also, notice any patterns that the day's log reveals. Did you spend too much time on the phone? Did you skip lunch because it seemed like you were too pressed for time? Write down some comments and observations at the bottom of the page.

Pay special attention to any obvious time wasters that show up during each day. What is a time waster? It's any shift of attention from a high-priority to a low-priority activity. If you were about to start on one of your six intentions, for example, but you were distracted by a casual phone call that took 30 minutes — that's a definite time waster. The first step toward eliminating time wasters is just to become aware of them. Sometimes just writing one down is enough to stop it. But other time wasters can be deeply entrenched habits that are difficult to break. As you begin to recognize those, you can incorporate breaking them into your six goals for each day. Write a brief description of the activity, along with its cause, a possible solution, and the date by which you intend to be done with it forever.

At the end of the week, see how satisfied you are with how you've spent your time. Have you fulfilled your goals and priorities? If not, you may need more focus in the week to come — or you may need to rethink whether these are really things that you want to accomplish. It's very important to be flexible. You're not a robot. You don't run on batteries or gasoline; you run on the primal energy that powers the Universe itself. By discovering your truest, most authentic desires and by taking control of your time, you can very quickly transform your life for the better. And time will be on your side.

Chapter Six

The *Principle* of *Sound* and *Light*

Part One: The Biology of Hope

You can master your innate personal power, glorifying exuberant vitality, exhilarating energy, and shining full spectrum balance, by understanding and using the Principle of Sound and Light. Sound and Light are literally the building blocks of all matter. Sound and Light create our entire physical world, and thus create each and every one of us. Sound and Light travel on parallel wave lengths, 40 octaves apart. In the physical world of matter, Sound precedes Light, as we know from hearing the thunder before we see the lightning in a storm.

By understanding and building upon your knowledge of the foundational significance of Sound and Light, you can revolutionize every aspect of your life. Sound and Light are the foundation of the Biology of Hope.

By understanding and using the Principle of Sound and Light, you increase the harmonious cooperative functioning of all the cells and physiologic systems in your body. Because we know that Body, Mind, and Spirit are different aspects of your unique unified being, this cooperative communication inside your body resonates with all the dimensions of your non-physical being.

We know that light, color, and sound have profound effects on all biologically regulated activities. Specific sounds and colors relax, soothe, stimulate and enhance metabolic functions, making them thousands of times more effective. Sound and Light evoke feelings, emotions, and therapeutic healing responses.

Ancient cultures used Sound and Light for many purposes, including healing. The Egyptians, for instance, created rejuvenating temples of Light. Native American, East Indian, and Aboriginal cultures used Sound and Light to cure illness, promote longevity, and integrate Body, Mind, and Spirit. Elixirs created by the Ancients captured the frequency essence of specific gems, across the rainbow spectrum of light. These elixirs are used today as a component of healing practices in India and many indigenous cultures around the world.

More recently, Sound and Light — in the form of MRIs, PET scans, CAT scans, laser surgeries, and noninvasive sound interventions — are important tools of modern medicine for diagnosis and treatment.

Each and every cell of our beings resonates a frequency that is in touch with every other cell in the body instantaneously — regardless of proximity. Each cell contains a "holographic blueprint" of every other cell in the body. Cells are as adaptive as they are unselfish: They are prepared to change, mobilize in emergency situations, such as an injury or bacterial invasion, and even die for the greater good of the body as a whole. So each cell can, if necessary, learn to sing the song of any other cell. The cells that make up our body demonstrate a wonderful model for peace.

WHEELS OF SOUND AND LIGHT

*"Every action in our lives touches on some
chord that will vibrate in eternity."*
– Edwin Hubbel Chapin (1814-1880)

All matter is created from subtle energy fields of Sound and Light. The radiance of Light originates from the Sun and is the result of hydrogen atoms pressed tightly together at the Sun's core.

The Sun releases and radiates energy in the form of photons that sustain the life forms on Mother Earth. The visible spectrum of Light and its relationship to Sound are intimately and reciprocally interconnected and interactive, far faster than the speed of light. The Sun produces Light, which when looked at through a prism, reveals the colors of the rainbow, red, orange, yellow, green, blue, indigo, and violet, and their various tones, shades, and hues.

Sound Health, Sound Wealth

All living things vibrate at specific frequencies. Because our bodies are composed of photons, we are literally "Beings of Light." Photons demonstrate their individual consciousness, depending on the circumstance in which they may manifest, either as a wave or as a particle. The atomic structure of your body demonstrates the dynamic intelligent arrangement of photons that vibrate into your very physical being. But from where have these measurable quanta of frequency waves of Sound and Light originated?

The actual meaning of the word *health* is "to make sound." Sound and Light interventions provide the most direct path to healing, maintaining a healthy *Resonance* in our bodies and optimizing our moment-to-moment experience. "First there was the Word" literally means that first there was Sound, an intelligent vibration.

Paramahansa Yogananda (1893-1952), in his discourse on The Christ Consciousness, spoke these words:

"The 'word' is the beginning source of all created substances in Cosmic Vibration imbued with Cosmic Intelligence. Thought of matter, energy of which matter is composed, matter itself — all things — are but the differently vibrating thoughts of the Spirit, even as man in his dreams creates a world with lightning and clouds, people being born or dying, loving or fighting, experiencing heat or cold, pleasure or pain. In a dream, births and deaths, sickness and disease, solids, liquids, gases, are but differently vibrating thoughts of the dream-

er. *This universe is a vibratory dream motion picture of God's thoughts on the screen of time and space and human consciousness.*"

The ancient Hindus believed that holy sounds, such as "Aum," "Ahh," and "Om," emanated from Spirit, that these Cosmic vibrations were simply the "frozen vibrations of Sound," from the luminous (Light) imagination of God, and that we are individualized aspects of those vibrations. According to these teachings, this vibratory force emanating from Spirit was endowed with the illusory power of Maya, or illusion. The Maya, or illusion, is that we are a compilation of solid matter, a body of bones, brains, and organs, when, in fact, we are each unique cosmic vibrations of the energy and intelligence of the Cosmos.

Since the inception of "humankind," we as a species have continued our quest for Light and enlightenment. The human species is the only species we are aware of that has learned to create and control Light. Early humans made sparks to create a burning fire. Candles and gas lamps followed, and, more recently, electrons were channeled into light bulbs and laser beams.

The Ancients knew, as do contemporary scientists and mystics, that we also have the ability to create "light from within," not only from neurological transmission of energy impulses, but from the Universe within each and every one of us.

THE LAW OF OCTAVES

Sound and Light are different manifestations of the same force, organized over and over again in a heavenly transformative process. In the 19th century, the mathematician P.D. Ouspensky referred to this as *The Law of Octaves.*

The word *octaves*, derived from Latin, means "composed of eight." Octaves have powerful organizing principles for Sound, Light, color, and life as a whole. Unfathomable magical and mystical possibilities exist through the manifestation process of the *Law of Octaves.* This is because the *Resonance* of our cells in the material dimension of observable matter is connected through the *Law of Octaves* to the fourth dimension, The *Quantum Hologram*, the Realm of the Miraculous, Spiritual illumination. Through this interaction, our focused thoughts and intentions become reflected back to us in synchronicities and even in the manifestation of material objects in the physical world.

THE EIGHT CHAKRAS

Six
The Principle of Sound and Light Part One

176

Imagine sunlight passing through a prism and dividing itself into seven pure colors of the rainbow, correlating to the seven musical notes on the music scale. These in turn correlate to eight whirling centers of energy in our bodies, which are known as chakras.

The Sanskrit word *chakra* means "wheel" or "disc." In the Northern Hemisphere, the vortices of these eight energy centers spin to the right, as if a clock face were placed on the front of the body. Chakras generally radiate out to approximately 12 inches in diameter.

I believe that the size, color, and sound frequencies of the chakras vary individually, from person to person, similar to the unique signature essence that characterizes each of us. In addition, the chakra system is influenced by situational factors. Your fourth chakra may be perfectly balanced in the morning — but if you encounter a situation that "hurts your heart," your fourth chakra will be affected, and become out of balance. Chakras may be rebalanced by changing your physiology through meditation, intention, nutrition, frequencies from both Nature and technology, and external energetic devices such as crystals or the sound of flowing water.

Our energetic, etherical bodies, connecting directly with the *Quantum Hologram*, are represented by our chakras. Each chakra resonates to a specific color on the light scale of physics, and has a corresponding musical sound frequency. Each organ, tissue, and cell, and the location of each, also has a specific vibratory frequency signature, which has physical, Spiritual, emotional, and archetypal *Resonance*. For example, healthy oxygenated blood is a bright red, whereas the liver's blood is purplish blue in color. Each individual chakra has a different color and a specific sound frequency vibration.

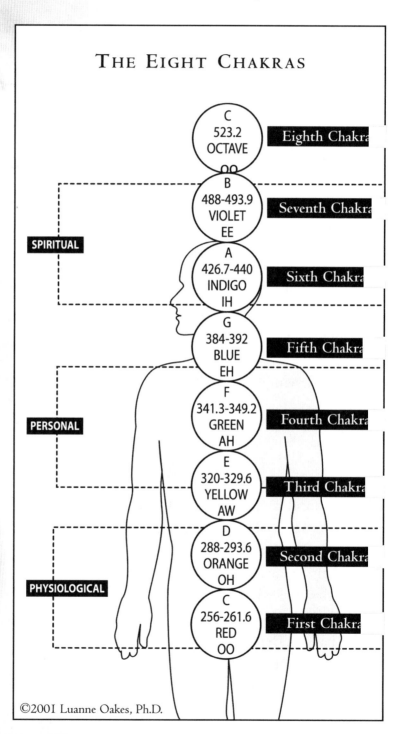

THE EIGHT CHAKRAS

C 523.2 OCTAVE OO	Eighth Chakra
B 488-493.9 VIOLET EE	Seventh Chakra
A 426.7-440 INDIGO IH	Sixth Chakra
G 384-392 BLUE EH	Fifth Chakra
F 341.3-349.2 GREEN AH	Fourth Chakra
E 320-329.6 YELLOW AW	Third Chakra
D 288-293.6 ORANGE OH	Second Chakra
C 256-261.6 RED OO	First Chakra

SPIRITUAL

PERSONAL

PHYSIOLOGICAL

©2001 Luanne Oakes, Ph.D.

There is general consensus that the chakra system begins with the First Chakra, called the "Root Chakra," at the base of the spine, and ascends to the Seventh Chakra at the crown of the head, although there are chakras or energy centers on the underside of both feet. Although there is a general agreement about the location and purpose of the first seven chakras, the number and exact locations of the chakras vary, according to both Spiritual traditions and cultural differences. Some researchers believe there is an Eighth Chakra above the head. For the purpose of moving sound and "toning" the chakras, I will refer to the basic unanimity of the findings.

It is important for us to understand the chakra system so that we can use sound and color in intentional and mindful ways to tone and balance ourselves. We as a species are highly intuitive, and you will know which colors to wear, which colors to place around you, which sounds to make, and what kinds of sounds to listen to, by what you are interested in and what occurs to you. Don't try to make this process too complicated or intellectual. Perhaps lie on the grass, look at the sky or a flower, listen to the birds — allow yourself to feel and know your intuitive way through this process.

As you experiment with making a variety of sounds, you will discover which sounds are just right for you and your particular situation. Some sounds may energize; others may calm you. I often vocalize sounds in my car with the windows rolled up, thus insuring the privacy of my sometimes very interesting production of sounds.

The *Sound Health, Sound Wealth* Frequency Treatments™ provided in the CD portion of this book are designed to effortlessly assist you with the process of tuning the very cells of your physical being, as well as brightening the Inner Light of your Higher Self. Please remember that in using the CD, some people become very relaxed, so the CD is never to be used while driving a vehicle or operating machinery. It may be played softly in the background at work or at home, or you might want to use as you gently relax into sleep.

The First Chakra resonates to the tones and shades of the color Red and to the musical key of C. This chakra is often referred to as the "Root Chakra," and is where the Kundalini (Life Force) energy is stored in its potential state. The First Chakra embodies our genetic imprint, survival, use of power, and groundedness (magnetic connection to the Earth's energy). Our rich red blood is the vibrant living river that delivers Life Force through the channels or vessels of arterioles, arteries, capillaries, and veins in our bodies. It is red because of its iron content. It is from this chakra that we become centered and grounded, or go into panic and survival mode. When performing primordial sound therapies, the Sanskrit seed vowel sound from ancient scientific wisdom for the first chakra is "Oo." You may notice the soothing effect this sound has on you if you gently practice sustaining both the sound and note (C), especially in a sacred surround, or in nature.

The Second Chakra resonates to the tones and shades of Orange and to the musical key of D. This chakra reflects individuation, ego, personality, reactive responses, and is located in the abdominal area. As you go through the process of individuation, or "leaving the tribe," you become the absolutely unique person that you truly are. This chakra denotes relationships as a whole. As children, moving through our early growth experiences, we begin, at first in small ways, to individuate from our parents, then those around us. If a parent, neighbor, or someone you are around is prejudiced in some way, you may find yourself reacting with anger, disappointment, and confusion, leading you to form your own opinions and beliefs about justice and related issues. The Sanskrit seed vowel sound for the Second Chakra is "Oh."

The Third Chakra resonates to the tones and shades of Yellow and to the musical key of E. This is the chakra of awakening. It is located directly through your solar plexus and thymus gland. The thymus gland is responsible for manufacturing interferon, interleukin, and other biochemicals with physical immune protective properties. It is also from this chakra that we develop our symbolic psychospiritual immunity from the negative thoughts and feelings from the world outside ourselves. The solar plexus is the chakra of integration. "Solar" refers to the Sun, and "Plexus," to bridge. It is the bridge (crossing over), the integrative synthesis of the First and Second Chakras, bridging the first two chakras of survival and individuation into the awakening of the heart. The Sanskrit seed vowel sound is "Aw."

The Fourth Chakra resonates to the tones and shades of Green and to the musical key of F. It is located in the chest region, including the heart and the lungs. This is the Heart Chakra. In Spiritual Alchemy, we learn to "think with our hearts." You have no doubt heard the saying "The Heart Knows." This is the chakra of reverence, mercy, harmony, and transcendence. The Heart Chakra is representational of Life Force in all forms. It is from this chakra that we create the energy for new healthy cell growth in all parts of the body. It is also the center from which we oxygenate ourselves through our lungs, on a cellular level. The Heart Chakra is where we receive oxygenation from the rain forests and all oxygen-giving flora on Mother Earth. It is from the Heart Chakra that we also create harmonious, loving relationships with all life. Its Sanskrit seed vowel sound is "Ah."

The Fifth Chakra resonates to the shades and tones of Blue and to the musical key of G. It is located in the throat region. This is the chakra of our emotional expression and creative response. It is from this chakra that we co-create, get into, and stay, "in flow" with Divine Source. When I was a child and young adult, I frequently had swollen glands and a sore throat, which I eventually overcame by expressing myself through Sound healing, singing, and telling the truth. The Sanskrit seed sound for the throat chakra is "Eh."

The Sixth Chakra resonates to the tones and shades of Indigo and to the musical key of A. This is the chakra of visionary response, enlightenment, Unity Consciousness, inner wisdom, and, like the Heart Chakra, reverence. In Spiritual maturity, our dualistic nature dissolves and Unity Consciousness flourishes. The center of the Sixth Chakra is located in the pineal gland, referred to as the "Third Eye," which is located almost precisely deeply between the two hemispheres of the brain. Its Sanskrit seed vowel sound is "Ih."

The Seventh Chakra resonates to the tones and shades of Violet and to the musical key of B. It is referred to as the "Crown Chakra" and is located at the top of the head. It is from this chakra that we receive our Visionary Response, Enlightenment, Inner Vision, and Intuition. Its Sanskrit seed vowel sound is "Ee."

The Eighth Chakra is the octave C, and it resonates to the shades and tones of Ultraviolet or White. Many believe the Eighth Chakra is located approximately 12 inches above the Crown Chakra — and that hundreds, perhaps thousands, more chakras ascend vertically, as depicted in many ancient texts. It is from the Eighth Chakra that a vortex of incoming and outgoing energy and information is communicated.

The color of the Eighth Chakra is usually not visible, although some people are actually able to see the colors of all the chakras. It is etherical in nature. The progression of musical notes through the chakras, beginning at the "root chakra at the base of the spine, to the crown of the head is as follows; C, D, E, F, G, A, B, and C, comprising the octave.

The Eighth Chakra is the Spiritual connection with Divine Intelligence denoting Love, Reverence, Revelation, Wisdom, Meaningfulness, and Understanding. It is from here that we receive our "Sacred Response," the clues and answers to our questions and quests. The Sanskrit seed vowel sound for the Eighth Chakra is "Oo."

Sometimes, when we create Sound, or listen to Sound, or bathe ourselves in color, or lose ourselves in the fullness of experience, we may connect with the *Quantum Hologram* and we are in flow. We are receiving a sacred response to the frequency of our own unique

Sound and Light vibrations. When receiving a sacred response, we sometimes feel overwhelmed by a feeling of unity with all creation. This is a wonderful and magical feeling. Having the intention of inviting more sacred responses, and allowing yourself to be assisted through higher frequencies of Sound and Light, enriches and enhances your every thought, feeling, and action, making everything more effortless. We are enlivened by a Power Greater Than Ourselves.

'MALILLUMINATION OF SPIRIT'

When we experience "Malillumination (absence of Inner Light) of Spirit," we feel a separation from a Divine Presence, Nature, God, or a loving Higher Power. Feeling left out, lonely, separate, and alone is reflected in our biochemistry. Stress hormones circulate through our systems and anxiety, depression, despondency, and even panic ensue. Situational or genetic factors, or a combination of the two, can activate these oppressive noxious feeling states. Whatever the specific cause, these feelings create a physiological pattern in the neuropathways of our bodies. As time goes on, the neuropathways of anxiety and depression, despondency and panic, can become more deeply embedded in the body, creating increased probability that these feelings will continue, and perhaps even intensify.

Mary was a lovely woman in her early seventies. She was experiencing advanced complications of diabetes. However, she told me her most serious problem had always been depression, and "not wanting to live." She had struggled with these feelings since childhood. Mary had been severely abused, beginning at the tender, innocent age of two. Her feelings of severe depression and wanting to die had existed since nearly the beginning of her life.

As I listened to Mary, I was deeply saddened by the horrific suffering she had endured, beginning so very early in her life. Her intense feelings had created physiological neuropathways and their corresponding biochemistry, which had endured over her lifetime. In other words, Mary's body unconsciously held injurious patterns on a physical level that had resulted in her feeling "bad" about herself and ashamed, leading her to isolate herself from others.

Mary had developed severe diabetes in her forties. Diabetes occurs when the pancreas and the liver become compromised in their ability to maintain healthy blood sugar and insulin levels. There are many causes of diabetes, including genetic predisposition, nutritional deficiencies, and, I believe, the body's inability to absorb and utilize minerals productively to maintain and enhance health.

One of the primary functions of the pancreas is to create enzymes from minerals, for digestion and tissue repair. Because of its centrality in blood sugar regulation, the pancreas is symbolically associated with the "sweetness of life." Mary's "sweetness of life" had been interrupted at a very tender and innocent age. Having survived through the years, assisted by good medical and psychotherapeutic interventions, she still had a very difficult time feeling trusting connections. Crying, she asked me if I thought she could heal her emptiness and feel in alignment with a fulfilling life purpose. After several visits to my office, Mary seemed different — more illuminated and alive. She told me that she was excited and surprised in a way she never had experienced in her entire life. She felt more connection to her real self and her dreams, more hope, and more physical energy, than ever before.

I had used Sound frequency technology and nutritional interventions to help Mary access and expand her Life Force. Of course, all her other therapies had laid the foundation for Mary's gains. I encouraged her to create strong "energetic boundaries" for people who drained her emotionally. I also asked that she monitor her pH, using medical testing strips that reflect the acidity/alkalinity of the body by utilizing saliva or urine. When Mary was around certain intrusive people who tried to force their "Ain't it awful" outlook on life on Mary, her body's pH became acidic, and she had to work harder to feel better, physically, emotionally, and Spiritually. The simple awareness that in taking gentle, deep, slow breaths she could actually nourish her Spirit made a notable difference in how Mary felt. It was empowering for Mary to know that she could actually measure the effectiveness of her changed and improved physiology and enhance her own "chemistry of consciousness" in a variety of ways: through her breathing, listening to Frequency Treatments™, enhancing Life Force nutritional intake, and creating better energetic boundaries.

Mary is still here on this Earth, and truly happy to be here for the first time in her life. She has literally been able to create "Light from within." She now directs her thoughts and feelings into beautiful poetry and stories. As she continues to *transform her life, she feels more "in control," and is happy, joyous, and free!*

If you find yourself in "Malillumination" circumstances, what interventions are correct for you? It is interesting to note that throughout history, serenity, peace, and healing of "Malillumination" may be assuaged without traditional, worn-out rules and dogma. Over the millennia, wondrous miracles have occurred that have assisted those suffering from these Life Force–depleting states. Overcoming lifetime or situational difficulties is very complex for most human beings. Although highly individualized, the ingredients for connection do seem to have some fundamental universal elements.

They appear to include, for example, <u>asking for help from a Power Greater Than Yourself, or any source in which you have Faith. Then reach out for assistance from a qualified healthcare professional</u>. It is also helpful to act "as if" you are already receiving help and guidance even if you are filled with doubt. Please make sure that you do make a connection with another person for assistance. It is often our egos that isolate us from asking for help and separate us from our Oneness with all life. Even if you are doubtful, you will receive assistance through synchronistic experiences when you truly have an intention to do so and if you give your attention to miraculous responses.

MIRACULOUS RESPONSES
ALWAYS ARRIVE

The following is a lighthearted example of how "assistance" arrived in a very unexpected way:

Many years ago, I was in a very beautiful but isolated wilderness area with my two dogs. I had a four-wheel drive and believed that when I parked in the snow, I would have no problem getting out when I wanted to leave. With snow-shoes on, I trekked through the forest with my dogs. The sun reflecting off the snow contrasted with the tall, vibrantly green pines. It was incredibly calm, still, and beautiful. I had packed snacks for the three of us, had a wonderful picnic, meditation, and exercise, but had misjudged time. Photons of radiant Light, captured in their "frozen state," made the landscape surrealistically bright and illuminated, contrasted by the dark but starlit sky.

When I finally returned to my vehicle, it was icy and my elderly Range Rover was literally frozen in place. I couldn't dig it out. We were either in for a long night of try-ing to hike out or of staying in the car. Since my cell phone didn't get a signal, I decided to have Faith and simply "ask out loud" for help.

Before I had even completed my request, my dogs became excited and began to wag their tails. Somehow they knew something was about to happen. Perhaps they were picturing the warm cabin and cozy fire that awaited them. But nothing was happening that I could see or hear. They continued to smile and wag their tails with joy.

Exactly seven minutes later, I saw a pair of headlights appear, seemingly out of nowhere. A woman pulled as close as she could get without getting stuck and asked if we needed a lift. In astonishment, I asked her why she was out in the remote area at that time. She said that she had been driving home and had suddenly had an impulse to drive down the narrow road, which by then had a foot of new snow. She said she thought that maybe someone needed help. She had chains on her "monster four-wheel drive" and said that she knew that she just had to turn down the unmarked road that was more like a wide trail. Climbing into her truck, I introduced myself.

To our mutual astonishment, we had been hearing about one another for years and had always wanted to meet. We spent a delightful and engaging time together while she drove me home. She came into my home and we enjoyed a long evening of conversation, dinner, and a cup of tea by the fire. This had a particular synchronistic meaning to me. I often think about people whom I would love to interact with, but I have a propensity to spend a lot of time alone in nature and in researching the vast and wonderful "World of Ideas." I do this whether I am at home by the cozy fire surrounded by my beloved books, or sitting and meditating on the beach. Very often, I do not take that extra step to set up a lunch date, although I think about it. In this instance, as with many others, synchronicity effortlessly fulfilled this desire for me. Ask, and you shall receive!

Sound Health, Sound Wealth

The Alchemy of Minerals and Crystals

*"You can trace every disease, and every ailment,
to a mineral deficiency."*
— Dr. Linus Pauling
Nobel Prize winner in the categories of both Chemistry and Peace

Minerals, which are crystals, each have their own unique and magical properties. Through Nature's munificence, enzymes are Alchemically created from minerals through Sound and Light frequencies.

Enzymes are Alchemical catalysts for vitality, transformation, and vibrant energy in every form. Enzymes are the Light and Life Force of our bodies. Enzymes and correct pH (acid/alkaline) balance keep our blood circulating, delivering nutrients and removing wastes. Natural enzymes keep blood flowing through arteries, arterioles, veins, and capillaries freely, preventing clumping of cells (plaque buildup) and inflammation.

Our bodies require minerals to create enzymes. Fresh raw fruits, vegetables, seeds, nuts, and juices are the most powerful foods that contain active enzymes. Enzymes act like cellular "pac-men" that break down food by ingesting, digesting, and preparing it for the elimination process. Our bodies are designed to move food through and be eliminated from alimentary canals within 12 hours or less. Wastes accumulate when this elimination process is slowed, leaving our bodies toxic, vulnerable, and with fewer immune defenses.

Over time, depletion of our Life Force enzymes creates serious problems of cellular degeneration and leaves the body with fewer immune defenses. Foods that are lacking in vibrant Life Force are packaged, processed, canned, heated (over 111 degrees), denatured, hybrid, and microwaved foods. When food is not organic and in its natural state, it often contains pesticides, larvacides, germicides, fungicides, metals, and other toxic substances in order to maintain appearance and shelf life. The suffix *-cides* means "poison." Hybrid foods often have had their nutritional qualities literally bred out of them for thicker skins, sweeter tastes, and longer shelf life.

The body, in its infinite wisdom, does its very best to assimilate nutrition from whatever we eat, as well as to neutralize harmful substances. Our bodies are always attempting homeostasis by storing toxins — accumulations of minerals and metals that are too large — as far away from our vital organs as possible, usually in our joint spaces. This creates inflammatory problems such as arthritis and gout, clogged lymph nodes, and peripheral nerve blockages. When these spaces become filled, toxic materials are then stored in the basement membranes of our cells, diminishing cell respiration, assimilation of nutrients, and elimination of waste products, and, finally, resulting in diseases of all kinds.

Mineral supplements have become very popular. In attempting to do the right thing for their health, many people are taking minerals and vitamins. These mega-doses accumulate in the "basement membranes" of cells, tissues, and joints. This is because although the cells of our bodies are constructed of colloidal minerals, colloids are absorbed into the blood but are often too dense (unless they are in a gas form) to be absorbed into individual cells. Heavy metal disorders can result from oversupplementation of minerals, in addition to environmental toxic exposure. Taking a supplement such as calcium is like eating rocks or chalk and asking your body to absorb them.

The best sources of minerals are foods grown in mineral-rich soils. When minerals have been distilled through the roots of plants, they are in their correct and balanced natural form, are rich in electrons, and, with the assistance of friendly bacteria, are transmuted from the mineral kingdom into the biological form that our bodies can absorb. Today almost anyone can learn to grow supernutrients, even if you're living in an apartment.

The mineralizing and growth process of plants can be greatly enriched by using preparations that are created for just this purpose from ocean water that has been collected several hundred miles off-coast, from over 200 feet deep. It is then concentrated and can be delivered to your doorstep. It may be mixed with filtered water to grow a small window garden or a garden in another small area with full-spectrum "grow lights." Grasses and ocean water are the best sources for a full complement of minerals. Many Life Force Nutritionists believe that of all vegetation, grasses contain the fullest complement of minerals. Horses, cows, and other animals that graze on grasses in sunshine have beautiful shiny coats and powerful muscles.

After taking doses of vitamins in the seventies for a time, I didn't believe in much supplementation, with the exception of Vitamin C from camu camu berries or other highly antioxidant plant derivatives. It felt safer to just eat foods in their natural states as much as possible. However, because of pollution and soil depletion, and after many years of practice and research, I now think it is important to use superconcentrated foods, such as Pure Synergy, Berry Green, or other organic supergreen products that contain organic neutraceutical-grade concentrated greens and berries. Bioavailable mineral supplementation is derived from biologically active plant sources and from sea vegetation. "Biologically active" means that they are vibrationally alive with electromagnetic frequencies that assist your body to propel them to your cells and to where they are most needed.

Many soils near ancient volcanoes in South America and in other places have magical properties, possibly from basalt in lava that is thousands of years old, mixed with remnants of rich rain forest vegetation. In many cases, foods grown in these types of environments contain atoms of gold and other minerals associated with biological "Light Consciousness."

The more vibrant the mineral, the more Light frequencies are available for the body.

Many health experts feel that 23 to 60 or so minerals are sufficient for maintaining health. Those who are interested in creating the biological environment for Light Consciousness sometimes ingest as close to 92 minerals in angstrom size as possible. Light Consciousness states are states in which life feels more full spectrum: You experience the enjoyment of higher vibrational thoughts, enhanced clarity and creativity, and availability of increased molecules of hope. More bioavailable minerals make it more effortless for our bodies to truly enjoy "Being of Light," biologically, mentally, and emotionally. It is very important to consult an expert when adding mineral or herbal supplements to your nutritional program. Some supplements should not be combined with others, and an experienced expert can also advise you of possible deleterious interactions with your prescribed medication regimen and specific dietary habits.

Demineralization of our bodies can cause deleterious and even catastrophic effects on our physical and mental health. I believe that demineralization leads to the separation from the Light Consciousness that orchestrates all life. Light Consciousness is not just a theory; it is a reality that affects each and every one of us. And as Albert Einstein said, "No problem can be solved with the same consciousness that created it."

ACTIVATING LIGHT AND SOUND WITHIN

Each atom of the Universe has its own unique *Resonance* or song. Spiritually, biologically, and physically. Sounds expand or contract. They <u>enfold</u> and <u>unfold.</u> The power behind our words, prayers, mantras, chants, and even our everyday conversations is created by the ways that Sound waves become organized. Sometimes we are "in *Resonance*," with certain people, places, and things. This *Resonance* may be positive or negative. We may also experience a magnetic attraction to a person, place, or thing that may not be a positive opportunity. By using our powers of intellect, as well as our feeling-based powers of discrimination in Body, Mind, and Spirit, we can better understand the real meaning of our attraction.

By using the *Law of Attraction* (like *Resonance* attracts like *Resonance*), you create the *Resonance* for that which you wish to attract into your life. Using the powerful Source of "free will" that we each have been given, we create our own orchestra of the many shades, colors, hues of Light; and the many Sounds, tones, and colors of our life experience, from within.

If you are more auditory in nature, you may wish to imagine that you are conducting the "Orchestra of Your Life." The instrumentation may be representational of what the Ancients believed were the basic elements of life: Fire, Water, Air, Earth, and Light. You can listen to actual recordings of the particular sounds that support and strengthen you. You can play an instrument yourself! You can re-create the Sound experience you enjoy in the privacy of your own mind. When possible, being in Mother Nature and her surround may be your first choice.

Fire may be represented by brass stringed instruments or brass or metal gongs. The Fire element may represent fulfillment of your intentions, financial freedom, physical energy, bright and interesting thoughts and feelings.

The element of Water, or major seventh piano chords, can be, as they are to me, like the ocean. You may automatically find yourself associating them with flow of synchronistic occurrences (messages from the *Quantum Hologram*), harmonious loving relationships with partner, children, friends, neighbors, and co-workers.

With respect to Air, woodwind instruments such as flutes and oboes are resonant.

Percussion such as drums of all varieties resonate to the Earth element, sounds of wholeness and completeness, assisting you to feel balanced, centered, and grounded.

Each section of your Sound and Light internal orchestra may represent feelings through Sound and Light that represent and activate different areas of radiant well-being, rich abundance, harmonious loving relationships, peace, and spaciousness. In regard to time and spaciousness, I recently have heard myself telling others, "So much to do and so much time!"

As we tune each area of our physical temples, we draw from the vast, unlimited, and timeless ocean of abundance, wisdom, and omnipotent Universal energy.

If you are a more visual person, you may enhance your internal environment of Sound and Light through photographs, paintings, imagery, or anything that activates Lightness, Sound, and Beauty.

If you are more of a kinesthetic (movement) person, you may activate and enhance your internal Sound and Light through movement that is soothing for you: yoga, sports, walking, stretching, singing, chanting, dancing.

THE *RESONANCE* OF SINGING

What comes to mind in regard to increasing your internal Sound and Light? Tibetan Master Djwal Khul said that *"There is nothing created in the world that is not energy in motion. We create what we desire through our thoughts, and every thought directs some aspect of that energy."*

Remembering that in and from this moment, here, right now, activating the *Law of Attraction* is continually resonating and reflecting back the vibrations of your thoughts, feelings, posture, physiology, words, and self-talk from and through the *Quantum Hologram*. This is why no matter what you have created in the past, you can begin to change in this very instant. Plant golden vibrational seeds of that which you wish to attract in your life. Imagine your cells actually radiating Light and vibrating with magnetic attraction. Singing is a very powerful way to support your biology, achieve balance, energize, and create a *Resonance* for attraction and manifestation.

It is often very helpful to repeat phrases to reprogram your very powerful Subconscious Mind, which is very literal and takes direction even when you don't fully believe a dreamed possibility. In fact, phrases become mantras when repeated thousands of times. New neuropathways are literally created and supported in your biology to facilitate and support these new structures. First, Sound vibrates into matter (subatomic to atomic ... then molecular ... to the cellular structures of your physical body).

You can begin by saying, singing, and chanting phrases of how you want to feel and that which you wish to attract. Do it with as much feeling and passion as you can with focused intention and conviction, until it becomes a habit. I believe singing and chanting can be very effective tools for moving "stuck energy" and for feeling better.

I once put the words of the Serenity Prayer to music. I simply made up a melody and it became a song. This was when my father died and I felt lost, exhausted, and sad. I remember walking through the redwoods and down a steep path to the beach. I just stood there in a thundering rainstorm alone, singing the prayer over and over, watching the huge waves crash on the northern coast. After about half an hour, a warm wave of peace imbued every cell of my being with peace, acceptance, and a deeper connection with my eternal self and Divine Spirit. While walking up the steep trail, I felt a renewed energy and strength. A sense of peace and "Oneness" beyond all description seemed to wash over me. I felt deeply loved and guided and felt a connection to Nature and all others.

Even when you don't initially feel like it, with enough repetition, you will usually begin to feel better — especially if you sing phrases or songs that you feel in your heart — melodies that move you. Make up ones that you love. Use language (perhaps new and interesting to you) with the intention of "Making Your Cells Sing." I still sing the Serenity Prayer. It doesn't make me feel sad but vibrant and alive. I reconnect with that lovely experience by the sea, and I am able to "feel it" again and again.

We all can benefit from singing from our hearts. I believe that everyone can sing and chant. It is a powerful way to activate our metabolisms, move blockages, and feel better. You can imagine harnessing the power of a thunderstorm, a bolt of lightning, the warm power of the Sun, the gentle emerald waves of the ocean.

Sound Health, Sound Wealth

Chapter Seven

The Principle of Sound and Light

Part Two:
How to Enhance Your Life Force

In the previous chapter, we began to explore minerals as magical structures that literally make our bodies vehicles of more Light. We need minerals in the correct amounts and in the right forms. Of the 92 or so minerals available on Earth, the cells of most people are severely lacking in the broad spectrum of "Light-Bearing" minerals. Nature, in her infinite wisdom, has provided us with the balanced mineral formulas that enhance our physical health and our brains' ability to function. Having an alkaline body illuminated with minerals of Light affects our entire brain function, and our enhanced brains are in instantaneous communication with each cell in our bodies. This interconnectedness allows us to maximize our Sound Health and Sound Wealth. One of the most important "Tools of Consciousness" for our ultimate health and well-being is magically created by our understanding and use of the principles of correct mineralization of our physical bodies.

The remainder of this chapter describes how Sound vibrates and Light radiates through the structures of our bodies and how we can literally enhance our Life Force by understanding basic concepts about how this works.

WE ARE BEINGS OF LIGHT

All living things, including us humans, vibrate at specific frequencies.

Because our bodies are composed of photons, we are literally *Beings of Light*. Photons demonstrate their individual consciousness depending on the way in which they manifest, either as a wave or as a particle. The atomic structure of your very being demonstrates the dynamic intelligent arrangement of photons that vibrate in specific ways, to create your particular body.

As mentioned in Chapter Six, the ancient Hindus and other philosophies believed that holy sounds, such as "Aum," "Ahh," and "Om," emanated from Spirit, that these Cosmic vibrations were simply the "frozen vibrations of sound, from the luminous (Light) imagination of God, and that we are individualized aspects of those vibrations.

According to these teachings, this vibratory force emanating from Spirit was endowed with the illusory power of "Maya," or illusion. The Maya, or illusion, is that we are solid matter, a body of bones, brains, organs, and skin, when in fact, we are each cosmic vibrations of energy and intelligence. Buddhist,

Kabbalist, Christian, and other philosophies alike, hold that we each are individual expressions of an immortal Divine Consciousness. Quantum Physics confirms this idea that we are composed of information packets of Light, bearing the illusion of appearing solid. In reality, the appearance of being solid is an illusion created by atoms colliding with one another. At the most fundamental level, we are fluctuating energy states that are "frozen in time."

ALL LIFE IS FROM THE SUN

According to scientists, the Earth began producing flowering plants 114 million years ago. Two million years ago, human beings made their appearance on Earth. The primary source of energy for all life on Earth is from the Sun. The Sun's rays energize the superconductor minerals that comprise all carbon-based life forms on Earth, including our bodies.

Have you ever found yourself lying on the beach, or grass, and, gazing up to the sky, you see tiny particles shimmering through the air? You may already know that these minuscule minerals are called colloids. They appear to swirl and dance to an unseen musical vibration.

Did you ever think of your body as anything other than solid bones and flesh? Physicists tell us that we are tiny particles of mineral dust that flicker in and out of physical reality and that we only appear solid.

Our bodies are made up of tiny dust particles known as colloidal minerals, combined with 70 percent water. <u>Within our bodies, minerals, which are crystals, reflect, refract and conduct Light</u>. Each colloid particle is equal in size to a wave length of visible light. The cell membranes of our bodies are literally composed of a variety of crystalline structures. These crystalline structures resonate, receive, and broadcast vibrational Sound frequencies throughout our bodies like a radio transmitter and receiver. Minerals emit different frequencies depending upon their atomic weight, which determines their Sound and color.

Looking in an anatomy book, you may have noticed that a healthy liver is bluish purple; the heart, a robust red; and the kidneys, a vibrant reddish brown. <u>The colors of our blood, organs, and tissues are determined by the colors of the colloidal minerals of which they are composed.</u> Because the cells of our bodies are continually replacing themselves, we greatly benefit by providing our bodies with foods that are mineral rich and bioavailable, that is, easily absorbable, for our very highest and best functioning.

LOW-FREQUENCY 'ERSATZ FOODS'

According to economist and author Paul Zane Pilzer, most of us are raised on sugary, salty, "ersatz" (false) foods. I certainly was! Our collective addictions to foods such as potato chips and processed cereals have been aggressively promoted by a food industry that calculates its sales campaigns by using the demographics, educational, and socioeconomic status of consumers, aiming for the greatest sales, with the least amount spent on advertising and promotion of the product. As Dr. Pilzer points out, the food industry has figured out that the best sales strategy for them is not to waste their money on attracting new customers, but simply to get its current customer base to buy lots more. According to Dr. Pilzer, a stated goal of one large food conglomerate is to get its target customer (a woman who already weighs 180 pounds) to buy enough of its product to increase her weight by 20 pounds in one year. Fortunately, largely in response to consumer demand, the food industry seems to be changing to promote higher-quality foods.

Chemical additives that are addictive neurotoxins are often found in "fast foods." In eating these foods, we often feel that we never get enough, so we keep eating more in an attempt to satisfy our food cravings. Unfortunately, most of these types of foods are biologically "dead." The rising number of obese consumers can be attributed to foods lacking Life Force. Many physical and psychological diseases and learning disorders and depression are exacerbated and sometimes even caused by improper nutrition. What our bodies are really craving are minerals that are only available from "real foods" in their natural forms.

Fresh, raw organic fruits and vegetables, soaked and sprouted nuts and seeds, and grasses (such as wheat grass) are the most bio-available source of the best nutrition. I believe that when eating cooked foods, it is best to also take very high-quality living enzymes, which are available at most health-conscious grocery stores. High-quality enzymes are absolutely necessary so that our bodies can digest, assimilate, and properly metabolize any cooked foods we may eat.

As Chapter Six explained, the best way to obtain minerals is through eating food grown in mineral-rich soils. When minerals grown in fabulous soil have been distilled through the roots of plants, they are in their correct, balanced, and natural form, rich in electron Life Force and, with the assistance of friendly bacteria, are transformed from the mineral kingdom into the biological form that our bodies can best absorb.

Because of demineralization and the overfarming of soils, ancient technologies are now being reintroduced into the agricultural fields. One of the terms for this type of farming is "biodynamic" farming, which was revived by educator Rudolf Steiner in the 1800s.

LIFE FORCE AND MINERAL-RICH FOOD

Now, almost anyone living in New York City, Tokyo, or Paris can learn to grow supernutrients — greens like wheat grass and a multitude of varieties of organic sprouts, all of which have unique tastes and fulfill different mineralizing functions.

As one ingests more bio-available minerals through fresh fruits, vegetables, nuts, seeds, grass-fed beef, free-range poultry, and deep cold-water ocean-caught fish, it becomes easier to enjoy a higher level of well-being, thus enjoying more vibrant energy emotionally, physically, and Spiritually. This is because the cells of our bodies are literally radiating, vibrating, transmitting, and receiving more Light, which in turn holographically enhances the pure potentiality innate within our bodies. The only long-term side effects are these: more optimism, clarity of thinking, creativity, "Lightness of Being," and better overall Sound Health and Sound Wealth. As an added benefit, foods that have a full complement of minerals not only help balance our bodies' pH, are more satisfying, and taste better, but also contain more particles of Light, which our bodies intuitively know how to use for cell, organ, and tissue repair.

CARNIVORES, OMNIVORES, VEGETARIANS, AND BREATHARIANS

Carnivores, omnivores, and vegetarians, alike, receive nutritional sustenance from the chlorophyll molecule. Chlorophyll molecules in plants function as "light banks" for photons. If you are not vegetarian, you are still nourished by chlorophyll, only in a secondary fashion, because animals are nourished by chlorophyll through ingesting, digesting, and metabolizing grasses and grains — unless they are fed an unnatural diet. Breatharians (there are very few to my knowledge) literally live on Light, some taking honey, or perhaps small amounts of water, a few times a year. Fruitarians receive photons stored in the cells of fruit, and, in some cases, also rely on sprouted (live) seeds. Some of the fruits highest in photons are mangos, papayas, pineapples, lemons, oranges, and avocados.

It is because of our subatomic makeup that literally living on Light is possible, although not probable, for most of us at this time. <u>Most of us enjoy the ritual of family meals and the tastes of many flavors of foods</u>. Unless we really understand why it is scientifically possible, many find the idea of Breatharianism preposterous. At one time, I certainly did, until I met one. He was practically living on Light.

LIVING ON LIGHT

In the 1980s after attending a class at the Holistic Institute in Santa Barbara, a small group of us met with a man who was a known Breatharian. He explained Spiritual Nutrition to us, and described in detail what was possible in the Cosmic transmutation of the energy of the Sun into electromagnetic frequencies that nourish the body's cells. <u>I was both skeptical and fascinated</u>.

The Breatharian gentleman was tall and very thin. He said that he drank only water once or twice a year, and sometimes had a few ounces of fruit juice. He had a beautiful complexion. If I hadn't met him through a very reputable friend who is also a Holistic Doctor, I might have had a less open mind. As I spoke with this Breatharian, while looking at his long, very lean arms, legs, and trunk, I finally voiced my concerns about his muscle strength and physical immunity. After all, it is our muscles, ligaments, tendons, and tissues that hold the skeleton together. The Breatharian patiently explained that he had plenty of strength and softly offered to demonstrate it. We walked down the stairs of the school and stood on the sidewalk, watching, as he strode over to a parked car, a Volkswagen Bug. He effortlessly lifted the car about a foot off the ground! My friend, Dr. Selinsky, later told me that he had seen this man lift more than eleven hundred pounds over his head.

Over the years, focused scientific study helped me develop a better understanding of how being a Breatharian might be possible. Although I must admit, at that time, the idea of giving up peanut butter, my sister's homemade Christmas cookies, or Mexican food had very little appeal for me. Our bodies perform Alchemy (biological transmutation) all the time. A successful Breatharian has simply refined the Alchemical process and is able to ingest Cosmic energy from the subtle energy fields of the Sun, Mother Earth, and other Cosmic forces to nourish his or her body. Most of us would rather enjoy sumptuous meals with friends and family, but it is interesting to contemplate the incredible powers of the Body/Mind.

I remember many years ago, Dr. Gabriel Cousens, M.D., Ph.D., in a conversation about the chemistry of alchemy, stating that, "The God energy is the ultimate food, and meditation is the digestive process."

Sound Health, Sound Wealth

Regardless of whether you design your diet based on body type, blood type, or any other approach that feels correct to you, the ideas presented here are simply "food for thought" in understanding how vibrations of Sound and Light are the foundational building blocks for all life forms on Earth.

I have had the great privilege of interviewing and working with many people over the last 30 years, focusing on emotional, Spiritual, and financial well-being, as well as on diet and nutrition. One gentleman, Dr. "R.," at 105 years old, was still enjoying vibrant energy and well-being, enthusiasm, and golf the last time we spoke. Before he semi-retired, Dr. R. was a Holistic Doctor, and also a minister.

I asked him about his dietary preferences and his secret to wonderful health and well-being. He told me that while at home he ate mostly an "Essene diet," a diet that consists of whole organic foods and sprouted grains. Having lost so many friends to "old age" and disease, he said that <u>whenever he was invited to dine with others, he ate whatever was put on his plate (including fast food) after saying a blessing of thanks</u>! He loves "breaking bread" or eating with his friends. No doubt his jubilant state of consciousness is because he is happy, having fun, and able to "transmute" and rearrange the atomic structure of whatever food he is eating. He lives his life with gratitude and joy while sharing as much love and humor as he can.

People often ask me what I like to eat. Over the years I have slowly changed the very poor dietary habits I had grown up with from birth, to eating raw organic foods 95 percent or more of the time. <u>I do, however, allow myself to eat whatever I really want without judgment</u>.

My choices stem from the fact that I simply feel better eating fresh raw organic foods. The benefits I have enjoyed are more energy, time, and creativity. I also enjoy the simplicity. There are some very amazing delicious raw food main courses and desserts that are incredibly tasty. I personally have no interest in preparing complicated meals. I drink a lot of fresh vegetable and fruit juices and eat a lot of avocados and concentrated "superfoods." Raw nuts are very handy. I always enjoy raw-food restaurants, especially on my annual visit to Kauai, where there are a couple of wonderful raw-food restaurants. I do find that chefs, everywhere I travel, are able to make a lovely plate with fresh garlic, olive oil, and fresh raw fruits and vegetables. Eating raw food contributes to plane-tary wellness because many of the environmental costs of fossil fuels and the release of carbon dioxide pro-duced by the feces of animals raised for market are reduced.

Before you make radical dietary changes, I feel it is important for you to become exquisitely aware of what you want to change and why you wish to change. If you need assistance, you can schedule a consulta-tion with a knowledgeable health professional, one whom you can feel "in *Resonance* with." <u>What works wonderfully well for one person can be very unbalanc-</u>

ing for another. Information provided here is simply, again, "food for thought."

RESONANCE WITH THE INNER OCEAN

When healthy, our bodies are composed of at least 70 percent salt water. The most abundant constituent of the surface of our lush emerald/sapphire-blue planet is sea water. Our beautiful oceans cover approximately 70 percent of our Earth. Beneath the surface, the oceans reveal vast ecosystems of sea vegetation, coral beds, and magically multicolored fish and other life forms.

To a surprising degree, human beings mirror the oceans in both content and form. Our bodies are like flexible vessels, 70 percent filled with salty water. The "sea life" and vegetation within our bodies consists of multicolored organs. The villi of our intestines, for instance, resemble swaying seaweed, absorbing nutrients created from symbiotic relationships with "friendly life forms" of bacteria. Both our inner and outer oceans are influenced by the Sun's warmth, the gravity of the Earth, and the Earth's magnetic fields.

The ocean, when healthy and unpolluted, maintains a healthy, balanced pH (the relationship of potential hydrogen ions and oxygen). Optimally, our inner oceans also maintain a pH of around 7.4. We must remain within a reasonable range of this pH in order to be healthy. When the pH of the internal ocean of our bodies becomes either too acidic or too alkaline, the fluid in our bodies becomes stagnant. If this persists over time, the life forms of our internal sea become diseased and eventually die.

To be in *Resonance* with our inner ocean, we must find ways in which to keep our acid/alkaline balance healthy, in order to facilitate intracellular communication through electrical conductivity. Our bodies actually function like a "wet battery." Although nutrition is very important, the acid/alkaline balance of our bodies is also significantly affected by the ways in which we cultivate and maintain our abilities to experience joy, fulfillment, and rich abundance in all forms.

Our bodies need to maintain a dynamic equilibrium of acid/alkaline balance. If the pH of our bodies becomes too acidic, we lose mental clarity, our cells become starved of oxygen, and we are then vulnerable to cancer and other diseases.

If we are too alkaline, we become irritable and develop muscle disturbances, and extremely severe imbalances may even lead to convulsions. Hyperacidity and hyperalkalinity are both dangerous states. Maintaining a healthy balance within a reasonable range of the ideal of 7.4 pH is the key.

Dr. Gabriel Cousens, M.D., Ph.D., has spent years doing scientific research and once said that the pH of foods can be classified by the ratios of potassium and sodium contained in particular foods. In his experience, foods high in potassium are usually alkaline, and those high in sodium are usually more acid. He refers to the alkaline/acid balance in the context of Yin (alkaline) and Yang (acid). He says, "The Yin and Yang balance of food is judged by such characteristics as their color, growth patterns, climate in which they grow best, height, density, and hardness. The color classification of foods is quite interesting; they are classified according to the color spectrum of the rainbow. The most Yang color is red, which corresponds to the base chakra, the energy center closest to the ground. The most Yin color is violet, which corresponds to the crown chakra, which is the greatest distance from the ground."

How does one maintain a healthy pH? Ayurveda is one of the oldest systems for individualizing dietary choices. Understanding our Body/Mind types in relation to the seasons and our vibratory Universe can also be very enlightening. There are literally thousands of books on physical health and related subjects. Regardless of which system you intuitively resonate to, it is important to remember that on the physical plane, for most of us, when foods are alive, they are naturally more alkaline, and, if grown correctly, mineralized. Foods need to be as organically pure as possible and to include the seven vibrational spectral colors of the rainbow.

Understanding the more universal dynamics to both our personal and collective acid/alkaline pH may be helpful in regard to creating more harmony both within our bodies and outside in the world in which we live.

In the ancient Oriental philosophical system, there is a timeless existence of a unifying dynamic relationship of the feminine Yin (shadow side of the mountain) energy, which is alkaline, and the masculine Yang energy (fire), which is acidic.

It is important to remember that Yin/Yang (alkaline/acid) principles are less about gender and more about balance. Males and females each must have both qualities in order to maintain a healthy pH. Balanced Yin/Yang energies are critical in the maintenance of our emotional, physical, and Spiritual well-being.

Yin principles, in both genders, when in balance, exemplify nurturing reflection, compassion, peace, joy, the connection to Earth and all life forms, and the recognition of Unity in Diversity. Yin (alkaline), when out of balance, leads to implosion, perfectionism, overinvolvement in the lives of others, and subversive attempts to control others.

The positive qualities of Yang energy are associated with fire and assertiveness, the ability to think clearly and objectively, to make and carry out plans, making life happen. When the Yang (acid) principle is out of balance, violence, destruction, oppression, and war ensue. These behaviors are often expressed in invasive, aggressive marketing, interpersonal war, and the destructive use of power.

pH testing strips can be ordered on the Internet or obtained at many whole food markets, and sometimes even in large drugstores. I prefer multicolored medical test strips. If you are interested, I encourage you to learn more about this subject. Utilizing your own innate intelligence, you may select from the menu of ideas offered here some simple ways in which you may confidently and safely monitor your body's pH, make correct dietary choices, and explore what works for you through your own *Magical Divine Experiment*™.

Efficient oxygenation and alkalization are critical in order for our bodies to have the internal environment to transport polluting synthetic molecules out of the body. We also need oxygen to perform critical functions on a cellular level to protect our bodies from illness and disease.

In 1931, Nobel Prize winner Dr. Otto Warburg discovered that cancerous tumors flourish in an environment that is deficient in oxygen. When the body is acidic and low in oxygen, cancerous cells are fed by lactic acid, a byproduct of fermentation. Oxygen and ozone therapies, widely used in Europe, are gaining popularity in other countries for the treatment of cancer and many other diseases.

Many people have negative neuro-associations to ozone because when combined with pollutants, such as smog, it is detrimental to health. However, ozone is potential oxygen and is one of Nature's bountiful gifts. It is created in electromagnetic lightning and thunderstorms. Ozone appliances (personal and commercial) for air and water treatments are easily obtained on the Internet. The ozone singlet attaches itself to the free electrons in parasites, tumors, viruses, and bacteria, and destroys them. Oxygen has two atoms, whereas ozone has three.

The most natural and simple ways to alkalize your body, in addition to nutrition, are to practice slow, gentle, and rhythmic breathing, meditation, visualization, chanting, and making sounds. Making sustained sounds such as the Sanskrit vowel sounds, "Aum," "Ahh," and "Om," open up the vortexes in the chakras, especially the Fifth, or Throat Chakra, which interacts and activates all other chakras. Enjoying sounds and sights of nature, Frequency Treatments™, and other related technologies also has tremendous benefits for keeping your pH in a healthy range. It can be tremendously exciting to discover what particular foods, sounds, thoughts, feelings, images, combinations of exercise, stretching, reading, and relaxing have beneficial effects on your pH. This journey of discovery may become an essential part of *Your Magical Divine Experiment.*

THE STRUCTURE OF LIVING WATER AND YOUR INNER OCEAN

To maintain your body and its "inner ocean," it is helpful to understand living structured water.

Sound Health, Sound Wealth

Thunder and lightning in storm clouds imbue rain drops with electron-rich vibrational Life Force energy. After the rain falls, it is absorbed into the ground. After traveling underground deep in the Earth, water works its way back to the surface into natural springs. In this form it is Yin, naturally alkaline. After water flows approximately 12 feet, it begins to create vortexes (whirlpools of water that spin clockwise above the equator, and counterclockwise below the equator). Then, the Yang energy of the Sun and air infuses the water with oxygen.

A beautiful place that I love to hike to every year is in a meadow between two snowcapped mountains. There is a deep stream, which becomes a small river. It is fed by the surrounding mountains as the snow melts. It is truly a magical expanse with a cornucopia of vibrantly colored wildflowers contrasted by green beautiful trees of the forest.

Every year, in exactly the same place, I am delighted to find a spinning vortex of crystalline water. I have actually recorded and used the Sound created by this natural phenomenom. I can smell the ozone created from the Yang oxygen entering the vortex of the Yin water as it bubbles and flows from the underground spring. The spring water is sweet, delicious, and refreshing. The journey of this water began as a blank tape as it recorded essential balancing messages and vibrations of Mother Earth — the memories of all carbon-based life forms, from all times.

When not polluted, this water from Nature is biologically alive with the frequencies of life from millions of years.

When we drink water that has been structured in this way, it is more biologically available to our bodies. The long chains of hydrogen bonds have been reduced, enabling water to enter the aquaporins of our cells easily. Aquaporins are angstrom-sized channels that allow water to flow into our cells. Structured water oxygenates, nourishes, and cleanses the cells of our being, helping us to feel better, more hydrated, and vibrantly alive.

Water is the magical elixir and universal solvent that eliminates toxins from our cells. Water is composed of oxygen and hydrogen, the most abundant atom in the Universe. Water is extremely important for the structural stabilization of proteins, lipids, and the membranes of our cells. Transportation of ions (charged particles) from cell to cell is possible only because of the presence of water in our bodies. Structured water reduces the extra expenditure of Life Force–draining metabolic work that must be accomplished by the body. Drinking structured water makes it easier to maintain good health. I believe the very highest and best sources of structured water come from pure rivers and streams (if available) and from "water rich" organic fruits and vegetables, because they are the most mineralized, alkalized, and ionized source of pure water abundantly available.

If I don't buy commercially structured water, I usually use distilled water, which is created by steam. It has the least amount of toxic contaminants and frequencies in it. <u>The problem is that distilled water is basically biologically dead and like a blank tape. The structure of distilled water must be changed so that the essential Life Force of the water is restored. For this reason, using a high-quality filtering system may be the best way of obtaining pure water for many people.</u>

There are commercial machines that ionize, alkalize, and purify your water. Again, if you're using distilled water, I believe it is important to find ways to make the water biologically active again. Healing practitioners and others, perhaps for thousands of years, have used various methods to imbue water with Life Force energy.

RESTRUCTURING DISTILLED WATER

For many years, I have used various methods to accomplish the restructuring of water. In our home we place huge crystals in the water dispenser itself and in addition add "microcrystals" (Crystal Energy) that reduce the surface tension of the water and assist in breaking down the long chains of hydrogen bonds. Our family enjoys writing messages such as Love, Peace, Compassion, on the container itself. This is a common practice to raise the frequencies of water. We also play "Frequency Treatments," such as the one included with this book, near the water.

Japanese researcher Masaro Emoto has photographed and documented the beautiful crystalline patterns created by the effect prayerful intention has on water; he has also documented the effects negative thoughts and feelings have on the structure of water. When the word "love" is written on a container of water, a photograph of the water cell shows a beautiful symmetrical pattern of organization, much like a unique snowflake. When the words "I hate you. I want to kill you" are written on a container of water, a photograph of the water cell shows a disturbing disintegrating shape, grayish, greenish, mottled, dripping off the slide. Our thoughts and words are things that always have feeling attached to them. Masaro Emoto's work graphically demonstrates this principle.

It is important to drink a lot of water. I usually recommend that you drink half of your body's weight in ounces every day in addition to eating large quantities of water-rich fruits and vegetables throughout the day. There are some medical conditions where this is contraindicated, and if you are not sure, it is wise to check with your doctor or healthcare practitioner.

CREATING AFFIRMATIONS AND INTENTIONS

To a large extent, regardless of what happens to us on the physical level of our lives, our minds and our hearts are the true co-creators of our life experiences. The nature of our lives is determined by the meanings we attach to events and by our ability to respond to them proactively rather than negatively.

As a part of *Your Magical Divine Experiment,* you can use every opportunity, seen and unseen, conscious and subconscious, to make yourself and the world a better place. To a very great degree, we each have the power to control our responses to whatever happens in our lives. When you activate this power, you may be surprised at the extent to which you can improve the physical events of your life — even discovering and making fabulous use of things that might have seemed like accidents or coincidences in the past.

To assist with this process, you may wish to try using the following affirmations. They are designed to redirect both your powerful Conscious and Subconscious Minds toward that which your heart truly desires. Read them through a few times until you've absorbed their meaning. Without any real effort on your part, the key phrases that are just right for you will be the ones you remember and make a part of you, with ease. Choose only those to which you resonate <u>or</u> create new ones that are just right for you. I created them for you. I hope you enjoy them.

I, _____, am a Radiant "Being of Light." Every cell of my being is Alive and Vibrating with Energy, Joy, Peace, and Hope, Now!

I, _____, Now only attract Wonderful, Harmonious Loving Relationships and Interactions with All Others. I am open and receive to Wondrous and New Synchronistic Opportunities, Now!

The cells of my being are literally vibrating with Peace, Joy, Laughter, and Hope. I radiate Love and it returns to me tenfold. All is well.

I, _____, am increasingly attracted to foods that nourish and rejuvenate my Radiantly Healthy, Vibrantly Energetic, Strong, Flexible, Youthful Body, Now.

I, _____, am Now Radiantly Healthy, Vibrantly Energetic, Lean, Flexible, and Strong! Every cell of my being is filled with the Golden Light of Peace. I am increasingly attracted to Vibrant Foods that nourish and rejuvenate every cell of my being, Now!

I, _____, let go of any and all toxic anger, resentments, criticism, and judgment of self and others, Now! I cast out of my being all "low-frequency toxic thoughts and feelings" to be completely dissolved and healed. I am filled with Love, Light, Peace, and Joy. I accept only the very highest and best always, and in all ways!

I, _____, Now attract to me people, places, and things that support my mission, purpose, dreams, and goals, in wondrous ways, I am filled with hope, Now!

I, _____, am open and receiving peace-filled and Inspirational Divine Guidance — Emotionally, Physically, and Spiritually, Now!

I, _____, am attracting circumstances, people, places, and things that are for my greater good as well as the greater good of all others, Now!

Multiple Rivers of Love, Joy, Peace, and Rich Abundance are cascading into my life and bank account here and Now!

Sound Health, Sound Wealth

*It is important to use the "present tense" in your affirmative statements. Your very powerful Subconscious Mind performs trillions of functions without one conscious thought. Your Subconscious Mind is very literal and is not restrained or confined to "collective time-bound awareness." Your use of the resounding power of your Subconscious Mind propels your wishes, dreams, and hopes into reality, Now!

Chapter Eight

The *Principle* of *True Wealth*

Sound Wealth Is True Wealth

"We must not try to fix the avenues through which our good is to come. There is no reason for thinking that what you give will come back to you through the one to whom you gave it."
— Charles Fillmore, *Prosperity*

SIMON AND SUZY BY THE SEA

I want to share with you one of my most treasured memories of something that happened when I was in my twenties — a series of events that created an ever-lasting foundation, deepening my belief and under-standing of what I think of as *True Wealth*. Within the core of my being, this experience in my early adulthood has generated, over time, a *Resonance* that has assisted me emotionally, physically, and Spiritually on the journey of my life.

Nearly every morning, just before sunrise, my elderly and deaf Dalmatian, Mickbookanook, and I would walk down the steep trail to the beach to meditate and play. For several years in a row, I couldn't help but notice the homeless man and his little white-faced black terrier mix. They always appeared out of the blue. Suddenly, they were "just there" for a few months, arriving about the same time every year. I would come down the trail and see that they had set up their small camp between two huge rocks, just far enough above the tide line to be safe from the surf when the ocean was rough. When the weather would turn really cold, they would disappear again until the next year.

He had only the sparest belongings: an old army knapsack, a couple of tin cups and a pot, and a very thin sleeping roll. He also had what appeared to be a tattered leather journal and a book or two. His clothing was very worn, even ripped in places. Once I had seen him take a swim, naked, while his dog sat on his jacket, looking worried and occasionally barking.

I would always nod or say hello, but never more than that until the year he arrived without his dog. Our eyes met, and I thought he looked sad. I took a deep breath and asked about his missing companion. He shook my hand, introduced himself as Simon, and offered me a cup of coffee. I sat by his campfire and joined him. The coffee was actually quite good. Simon told me that Suzy had finally gone to The Good Lord. I offered him my very heartfelt condolences and told Simon that I was sure he must miss his little Suzy. He did. His eyes welled with tears as he petted my dog.

Simon began to speak, answering questions I wouldn't have dared to ask as he told me a bit of his life story. Our conversation that day focused synchronistically on the topic I had been almost obsessively intrigued by for the previous three years: Prosperity. In 1929, Simon, like many people, lost a significant amount of money in the stock market crash. He told me that a few of his closest friends had committed suicide; one had even jumped out of a high-rise building to his death. Shortly after the crash, Elizabeth, his beloved wife, had died unexpectedly. Simon told me that he had sold their home and embarked on a very different lifestyle that suited him "just fine." Other than his deep sadness about the loss of his wife and his little dog Suzy, Simon didn't seem unhappy or depressed in any way. He said he loved his life and that he had never worked another day after the loss of his Elizabeth. He told me they had no children.

The following morning I brought Simon a bag of coffee, some bagels, and a large, warm sea foam green-jacket that I had received for Christmas but had never worn. I also gave him my last 20 dollars. He thanked me and said he always received what he needed, and just when he needed it. He asked me if I was sure I could afford it. It was almost funny; I could barely afford to give him the money, but I knew it was the right thing for me to do. It was my last 20 dollars in cash. I had to use my credit card to buy groceries.

Simon made no apologies for his life as a tattered elderly homeless person. He seemed well read and said that bookstores all over the country had free books and that when he finished a book, he left it behind, replacing it with a fresh new one to begin. Simon radiated health, optimism, wisdom, and vitality. I had often seen him reading, and he didn't wear glasses or squint.

He told me that his money from the sale of his and Elizabeth's lovely home had run out more than 40 years ago but that his needs were always more than met. He also said that he had never asked anyone "for a crust of bread" and that he was always provided for. At first I thought of his way of life as frightening and depressing, but that obviously was not his experience.

Simon told me that he defined True Wealth as an "inside job" and that he knew he would always have food and shelter whenever he needed or wanted them. He told me that once he had established this idea of True Wealth in his heart and mind, he had no fear and lived entirely by Grace. Obviously, he had many years of experience of practicing his Faith.

Simon said that except for his relationship with his wife, he really hadn't missed "the fast life," as he called it, though he had thought it was enjoyable at the time.

At first I felt petty and superficial as I shyly told him about the Prosperity Seminars I had been attending and how I had been struggling with the whole concept of money and wealth. I also admitted that I wanted to experience money and wealth, and lots of it. He said that in his opinion that was all fine, as long as I understood that the Divine Presence of God would never judge me either way. He said, "There is absolutely nothing wrong with having money and material things, as long as you don't get too attached to them. Money comes and goes. Inner True Wealth is something that you need to lay a sound foundation for, inside yourself, and never, ever lose it, because it is Spiritual in nature." Simon said he had enjoyed many material things and that if he wanted them again, he could certainly attract and create them. He didn't seem to want them though. Simon said he never in a million years thought he would end up living the way he did. He had only meant to "bum around" for a year or so when his wife died. "That was a very long time ago," he said.

"True Wealth," he told me, "is a philosophy. It's how you treat others, how you take care of yourself, and learn to give as much as you receive, or actually, give more than you receive. Having gratitude and fun every day is important too." Simon seemed well adapted to the life he was living. He told me he enjoyed watching each sunrise and sunset from the many different places he traveled. He said that he attended church, synagogue, or Vedanta temples sometimes, and added, "I always have just the right person to talk with when I am feeling sociable." He winked at me with his brilliant, sparkly azure eyes, lighting up his wrinkled tan face. Simon's message to me was powerful. He talked about The Law of Giving and said, "When you give in the proper way, it feels just right in your heart."

Simon asked me for my address so that he could drop me a line, and perhaps send me a postcard. I wrote down my address and gave it to him. That was the last time I ever saw Simon. Maybe he took California off his travel itinerary.

About two years later, I received a thick manila envelope, postmarked from the Gulf of Mexico. There was twelve hundred dollars, in tens and twenties, in the envelope! On the enclosed postcard was scribbled, "Thank you for being a light in my life. Never lose your faith in *True Wealth*. And never change from being the truly kind person you are." There was no signature. I felt sure the envelope was sent to me by Simon. The tangible reminder of the connectedness that Simon and I shared brought tears to my eyes. Oddly enough, I had thought about Simon just the night before. Around midnight the previous evening, a bright, starlit night, Mickbookanook, my beloved old

Dalmatian, had died in my arms. While I was soothing and comforting him, he slipped into a coma; I had thought about Simon and Suzy. The next day, around noon, I received the envelope.

I began giving money more frequently, using Simon's wisdom. I gave anonymously, often with a message of thanks, sometimes offering encouragement.

CREATING *TRUE WEALTH*

True Wealth is a state of well-being in which, regardless of outward appearances and circumstances, you develop an "inner knowing." You have total certainty that you are attracting and creating all that you need and desire, including money. Your inner knowing that you are creating all *Your Heart's Most Treasured Desires* actually results in the outward manifestation of all that you need and want, in ways that will absolutely astound you. The external world will actually manifest *Your Heart's Most Treasured Desires*, mirroring the microcosm, your inner world, when you practice the *Principle of True Wealth*.

The *Principle of True Wealth* works so effectively because it honors and respects the self, the world, and all others. Everyone, every living being on the face of the Earth, benefits when you practice the *Principle of True Wealth*. This is because the *Principle* is based upon venerable ethics, honorable behavior, and inclusive morality. In this context "inclusive" means that this

Principle is available to all who wish to use it for the greater good of themselves, of all other beings, and of the Earth itself.

The *Principle of True Wealth* consists of the following:

- Being in the present moment

- Being in *Divine Flow*

- Frequent experience of Compassion, Reverence, Love, Peace, Joy

- The ability to forgive

- Giving without attachment to the outcome of your giving

- Certainty that *We Are All One*

- Certainty in a Power Greater than Yourself

- Certainty that there are enough resources for every man, woman, and child on this Earth to have all their needs met completely and fully

- The ability to accurately assess your own and others' strengths and weaknesses, in order not to project your own dark qualities onto others in the form of prejudice, stereotyping, or blaming

- The ability to be grateful for something, at least once a day, no matter what your circumstances

- The ability to reduce the intensity of negative thoughts and feelings, and change your "first thought and feeling," if it is negative or destructive in nature, into your "second thought and feeling," which will be positive and constructive

Sound Health, Sound Wealth

Each of us must fine-tune our own definitions of exactly how we live the *Principle of True Wealth* in every hour, minute, and moment of our lives. A valuable practice to assist your dreams in becoming your reality is to write down each and every desire you hold in your heart. Be sure to include your personal dreams, as well as your dreams and desires for all others and for the world. As you read this over, allow yourself to experience in full detail all the positive feelings that are attached to each of your dreams and desires, for yourself, those around you, and the larger world. Writing your desires and endowing them with the feelings that accompany your dreams creates a template through which you will attract your highest good. This facilitates the transmutation of leaden thoughts into golden realities. Keep this list close to your heart, and read it often.

As the *Principle of True Wealth* comes to reside in your consciousness, they will begin to function more and more automatically. When your Conscious and Subconscious Minds work together cooperatively, you begin to consistently engage in the *Principle of True Wealth* by practicing it each and every day with your whole being.

WEALTH VERSUS GREED

"A gift with reservations is not a gift; it is a bribe.
There is no promise of increase unless we give freely.
Let go of the gift entirely.
Recognize the universal scope of the law.
Then the gift has a chance to go out
and to come back multiplied.
There is no telling how far the blessing
may travel before it comes back.
It is a beautiful and encouraging fact that the
longer it is in returning, the more hands it is
passing through and the more hearts it is blessing.
All these hands and hearts add something to it in its substance.
It is increased all the more when it does return."
– Charles Fillmore, *Dynamics for Living*

What often disguises itself as life satisfaction and *True Wealth* is, in fact, greed. The definition of greed is "Excessive or rapacious desire, especially for wealth or possessions." Greed is an energy-draining, low-frequency state, based upon underlying beliefs in limitation and lack — that there are not enough resources for everyone to have their needs and desires met more than adequately. It is no wonder that many of us have experienced constricted channels of Flow, historically or presently, if we have negative neuroassociations that confuse wealth with greed.

The subatomic and electromagnetic frequency of greed is the opposite of Faith. Greed eventually leads to constrictions in all areas of our lives, physically, emotionally, and Spiritually. Greed closes up the channels of *True Wealth* when we are dishonest, take more than we need at the expense of others, or take without considering the needs of others.

LIFE SATISFACTION AND *TRUE WEALTH*

We all experience Life Satisfaction to the degree that we feel fulfilled, gratified, and content at any point in time. *True Wealth* is both the most significant determinant of Life Satisfaction, and, most importantly, the most direct path to achieving it. Interestingly enough, neither *True Wealth* nor Life Satisfaction is directly related to social status, education, occupation, material possessions, or even physical health. *True Wealth*, at its very core, is the ability to enjoy a peaceful relationship with one's self, all others, and the world.

True Wealth is accessed through Faith. Although "Faith" is not listed on the New York Stock Exchange, it is perhaps the most precious and valuable commodity that exists in the Universe. Faith is an energy, feeling, and frequency in our body/minds that becomes an actual energetic arrangement, a specific molecular configuration fostering the biochemistry of calmness, serenity, peacefulness, contentment, creativity, compassion, and love.

My definition of Faith is "Belief, not based on objective proof, that things will turn out as they are supposed to." This definition of Faith implies acceptance that we cannot and should not attempt to control others, that others have the same rights and pre-rogatives that we want for ourselves, and that there is a larger plan in the Universe that we may not under-stand in its wholeness. Imbued with this kind of Faith, we all may enjoy more peace in our hearts. As we develop our Faith, it becomes an ever-deepening well from which we may draw calming and soothing states of being — serenity, strength, optimism, and peace — even in moments of greatest adversity.

THE FOUR NOBLE TRUTHS

Whether knowingly or unknowingly, Simon had reintroduced me to the Buddhist precepts known as The Four Noble Truths.

History tells us that the former Prince Siddhartha Gautama, born near the foot of the Himalayas around 500 B.C., left the comfort and safety of his palace to inform himself about the realities of how his people lived. He discovered poverty, suffering, and depriva-tion of many kinds. He sat, observed, and meditated on what he believed might be the "middle way, the way of living that would be neither grandiose narcis-sistic wealth nor abject poverty and suffering."

One day he appeared from the shade of the trees along the plain of the Ganges River after years of observation and meditation. Now he was the Buddha, The Enlightened One, with his philosophy of The Four Noble Truths:

There is suffering in the world, whether mental or physical.

<u>Suffering occurs because of too great an attachment to one's desires.</u>

By eliminating attachment, you can eliminate suffering.

There is a method to eliminating the cause, called *The Eightfold Path*, a guide to "right" behavior and thoughts. *The Eightfold Path* is a moral compass leading to a life of wisdom (right views, intent), virtue (right speech, conduct, livelihood), and mental discipline (right effort, mindfulness, concentration).

Buddha provides us with an inspiring model for giving without any attachment to the outcome of our gift. He also serves as a compelling example of Faith. He left his palace on a journey that required the deepest Faith that things would turn out as they were supposed to.

GIFTS OF LOVE AND ACKNOWLEDGMENT

Although I have always donated to charitable organizations, ever since I met Simon, I give most of my contributions secretly to those who have nourished me Spiritually, or sometimes, to those I don't even know. Giving in this way, for me, is more fun and rewarding because I let go of my attachment to giving, expecting that I will get something, even a letter of acknowledgment, back.

Over the years, interestingly enough, I have received hundreds of envelopes enclosing money, with mysterious heartfelt messages of gratitude and encouragement. It's a mysterious fact that I have never knowingly met any of the people who have sent these gifts of encouragement. When Europe changed its money system, I received my first euros in this way. I treasure their meaning too much to spend them, although I must admit that sometimes the sacred money I have received in the mail has arrived at just the right times, when I have needed it most.

From Simon, I learned to define my own personal meaning of *True Wealth* — remembering on a daily basis the things that are most important to me. They include having fun every day, nurturing harmonious, loving relationships with Divine Spirit, people, and animals, researching my many interests, reading, enjoying walks in nature, making a difference in someone else's life through a message, phone call, or a gift of my time, and other simple pleasures of daily life: movies, books, music, meditation. I value a quiet "un-busy" life.

THE BIOCHEMISTRY OF *TRUE WEALTH*: MAKING YOUR CELLS SING

What do you believe about life, relationships, wealth — and money? Do you believe that money is the root of all evil? Whatever you believe about Life Force in the form of money will make it so. When all else fails, think like Jesus, Buddha, Allah, Divine Presence, or God. What do you imagine an Ascended Master would do in a specific situation of real need? Of course, you know the answer to this question. Ascended Masters, long before they cross over, create whatever they need for themselves and others in difficult situations. We, you and I, can create whatever we need both for ourselves and others when we follow the *Principle of True Wealth*.

I know that the Universe will stand behind you in whatever you believe and pursue — especially if your desires include the highest and best for all others. This is because when we include others in our highest and best thoughts, our cells literally light up, and all parties — those who give and those who are receiving — are enhanced with a higher *Resonance*. When we give, especially in ways that Spiritually support us, we receive back exponentially. If you give material things, you will receive material things; if you give love, you will receive love; if you give of your time, if you offer compassion, love, understanding, and grace, you will receive them back, more than tenfold. It is my experience that when you have given from your heart, your cells literally sing with joy and bliss!

TRUE WEALTH THROUGH DIVINE FLOW

The biggest challenge for any of us, I believe, in creating *True Wealth*, is to remain in Flow, *Divine Flow*. Because we humans and everything else on our planet vibrates into Beingness though energy, information, and intention that issues from the Divine Field of the *Quantum Hologram*; our physical bodies supply us with a microcosmic model of *Divine Flow*. Our Earth also offers us continual demonstrations of the miracle of *Divine Flow*.

There is a natural "Flow" of movement, circulation, vibrancy, and vitality in nature. Waterfalls, rivers, rainstorms, and ocean waves, naturally, flow. Water remains biologically alive and pure when it is flowing. The same is true with our bodies and every aspect of our lives.

It's truly inspiring to think of our bodies as an internal landscape, a microcosm of Mother Earth, in which we also have natural rivers that flow, through our blood and lymph systems. When Flow is constricted in any way, and for any period of time, we experience contracted congestion, tightness, pain, and, if unchecked, illness. The same is true in all areas of our lives. One area affects all other areas of your being. If you are constricted emotionally, the narrowing of Flow will affect your body, your mind, and your Spirit, just as a constriction of Flow in your body will affect all other areas of your functioning.

Divine Flow is a mysterious sense of precious connectedness, in which we enjoy a sense of transcendence, often feeling a mystical experience of Universal Harmony. We may enjoy this magical state almost anywhere, in the workplace, picking up trash, or stepping onto a commuter train. This is because *Divine Flow* is a transcendent state of being; that which might usually feel ordinary or mundane, even perhaps somewhat disgusting or noxious, is transformed, because we are at peace in present moment, One with the Universe.

Having the intention to be in Flow, with whatever is being presented to us, eventually works, if we cultivate Faith and persistence. It is often persistence that precedes Faith, and not the other way around. The bonus is, when we are in Flow, we are extraordinarily better able to deal with difficult situations.

Dr. Mihaly Csikszentmihalyi, who has extensively researched the many aspects of Flow, has said, *"Of all the virtues we can learn, no traits are more useful or more essential than the ability to transform adversity into an enjoyable challenge."*

AN INNER INVENTORY

Where in your life are you experiencing a constriction in *Divine Flow*? The following checklist can help to identify areas and ways in which your Sound Wealth and well-being may be affected. By taking an inventory of where we may have a "constriction of Flow," in our bodies and in our lives, we may open blocked or narrowed channels of energy that may be impeding the ways in which we experience health and well-being in our lives.

Physical Well-being:

Are you feeling an interruption of Flow through tightness in any area of your body, pain in your neck or back, difficulties with digestion, absorption, or elimination, frequent colds or flus, illness, lack of vibrant vitality and energy?

OR

Do you engage in regular physical exercise, appropriate to your body, that you look forward to and love? Do you nourish your physical being in ways that are respectful and healthy for you?

Emotional Well-being:

Are there resentments you hold toward others, or resentments held against you? When we don't acknowledge our own "dark side," it is easy to project our own unhealed issues onto others by projecting blame, prejudice, and stereotyping.

OR

Do you feel love for yourself and others? Do you feel loved, appreciated, and in *Resonance* with all those in your personal life, and, as appropriate, in the world around you? Do you have fun every day? Do you laugh frequently, with exuberance and joy? Are you able to make an accurate assessment of your strengths and weaknesses, one that the three people who know you best would agree with? Are you able to spend a lot of your time in present moment? Are you open to novelty and adventure, of whatever kind is appropriate to who you are and who you want to be?

Spiritual Well-being:

Do you feel forgotten or insignificant?

OR

Do you feel safe, protected, and in *Resonance* with a Power Greater than Yourself? Do you feel you can call upon this Divine Presence or God for assistance and guidance? Do you have fun, laughter, and freedom every day?

Financial Well-being:

Are you in debt? Do you feel overwhelmed, ashamed of your financial situation? Do others speak of their retirements, while you are struggling to survive? Do you believe that if you have more, then others will have less?

OR

Do you feel empowered in regards to financial wealth? Are you able to provide health care for yourself, your loved ones, and even strangers? Do you believe if you had more, you could help others more?

'LETTING GO' RESTORES FLOW

Just as water must flow to remain biologically active and pure, so too must our lives, internally and externally, Flow, in order for us to function at our highest and our best. By removing obstacles that block Flow, we free up and open significantly wider and deeper channels to both receive and give abundance.

In the early 1900s, the psychiatrist William D. Silkworth, together with Bill Wilson, created a self-help program that is Spiritual, but not religious: Alcoholics Anonymous. The philosophy in its purest form assists one to heal through turning one's life over to a Power Greater than Oneself. The necessary abstinence for recovery from alcoholism and other addictions is accomplished through a "mystical experience," the essence of Unity Consciousness: knowing there is a Power Greater than Ourselves (whatever it may be), and that *We Are Not Alone.* It is fascinating that the Twelve Step philosophy used by Alcoholics Anonymous has one of the highest rates of success in treating addictions of all kinds, worldwide. It is also free. For many people, Twelve Step programs help restore Flow through the practice of forgiveness and "letting go."

In this context, learning to forgive and let go is a process of nonjudgment and detachment. You release the "energetic connection" to what happened in the past, become accountable for hurtful and destructive behaviors toward self and others, releasing the outcome of this process to a Power Greater than Yourself. Letting go allows you to move into present moment, thus re-establishing Flow. Forgiveness through detachment in no way condones evil or destructive behaviors in the past, present, or future.

HEALING SEPARATENESS

Who among us cannot look back on some of our actions in the past and wonder why we ever engaged in behavior that was not in our highest and best interest? At least many of us have engaged in behavior that was impulsive, ill considered, perhaps even negative for us in some significant way. Some of our human behavior is compulsive to the point that it is destructive or damaging to ourselves or others. Such behavior is actually our attempt to "feel better" and to heal the separateness we may feel from ourselves, each other, Nature, God, or a Power Greater than Ourselves. We sometimes attempt to heal our unbearably painful separateness by creating a "feeling state change," through the use of alcohol, drugs, "being right," "being perfect," overeating, sex, gambling, work, exercise, relationships, or incessant cleaning or watching the news. We thus become numb, jaded, even frozen. We no longer believe that we have the ability to make a difference in ourselves or in the world.

A few hours of recreational time spent watching television, playing video games, or surfing the Internet probably has no real negative consequences for any of us. However, significant numbers of hours per week spent on any activity that becomes obsessive or compulsive may result in our separation from our innermost selves and all others. We lose heart, and we lose hope. Any type of compulsive behavior creates an energy field of false protection. Judgment, anger, resentment, and unforgiveness of self and others can be addictive, especially if we can feel right and believe that others are wrong.

By staying in these patterns, we often avoid the deeper issues, including our own accountability for what is happening in our immediate situation and in the larger world. It may appear to be easier to blame other nations, our own government, our co-workers, parents, children, spouses, partners, neighbors, and other races, religions, and belief systems than to take responsibility for what we can do to change what we don't like. I am not saying that we don't need to take appropriate actions in regard to crime and violence. It is, however, not in our own best interests to focus on what is wrong with everyone and everything else. What we do have is the power to change ourselves. If enough of us change ourselves, the world will change as well. Admitting that we have become powerless over a substance, person, place, thing, or situation opens the golden door for Divine Assistance. We can then heal our felt helplessness and seeming hopelessness, resolving a painful adaptation to avoid pain that may have turned into a frequency of avoidance.

CALLING YOUR SPIRIT BACK TO YOU

In this moment, imagine that a disturbing situation was resolved and *Your Heart's Most Treasured Desires* were already manifested. How would you sit or stand, and breathe? Would you have a smile on your face, a sparkle in your eyes? What language would you use in your mind and in conversation with others? Imagine your relief if you enjoyed more harmonious loving relationships, were debt free, had plenty of money in the bank, had plenty of time to read, learn, paint, do nothing at all, knit, draw, walk, hike, ski, or whatever it is that you might wish you had more time for? Would you feel tremendous relief, joy, contentment, excitement, happiness, peace? More than likely, you would feel like your most authentic self, your very essence dancing with delight, fully in the moment, One with All.

One of our most powerful techniques for calling our Spirit back to us and living our dreams is our ability to change our very physiology through constructing our consciously chosen second thoughts and our second feelings. We thus instantly change our internal world, which, in turn, impacts the larger world around us.

Although we cannot always have wonderful first thoughts or feelings, we can consciously choose a higher vibratory thought or feeling to replace anything not in our own best developmental interests. By consciously re-choosing our thoughts, we send a magnetic message to the *Quantum Hologram*, attracting the events and opportunities that will enable us to effortlessly solve our current challenges.

Can we actually choose our thoughts and feelings? The answer is a resounding "Yes!" As mentioned earlier, you cannot necessarily choose your first thought or feeling. Thoughts and feelings often arise unbidden, seemingly out of nowhere. You can, however, choose your second thought and your second feeling, replacing fear with Faith, depression with hope, anxiety with serenity. In this process, you empower and reconstruct yourself. Of course, it is absolutely necessary for you to know what you think and feel in order for this scientific magic to work for you. In fact, it takes a lot less energy to practice this "scientific treatment," than it does to continually review and replay troubling situations in your life.

When we change our thoughts and our physiology, we find new solutions because we have new and empowering thoughts, and as Napoleon Hill taught, we make better use of "The Gold Mine" between our ears, "to re-create our ever-improving life experience." We may then make newer and better choices in all areas of our lives. This may include diet and exercise, leading to our rejuvenated, enthusiastic, and "vibrantly changed biology," spiraling upwards, creating higher and higher frequencies of functioning. We may then harvest the dreams and goals we had previously not yet imagined because our view was blocked. Our significantly improved thoughts and feelings become our new life-enhancing beliefs. More and more effortlessly opportunities of rich abundance are flowing to us each time we engage in this mindful practice.

When we call our Spirit back to us from inappropriate people, places, things, old beliefs, "low-frequency" fear-based thoughts, and ideas that no longer serve our highest and best, we open the omniscient channels of *Divine Flow*. Where do you want more *Divine Flow* in your life?

INNER AND OUTER ABUNDANCE

Unbalanced competitive behavior robs us of our own originality, creativity, and present-moment awareness. Unhealthy competition is based on the assumption that there is a finite, fixed, and limited amount of resources — nothing could be further from the truth. Competition is characterized by a win/lose mentality. *True Wealth* is based on a win/win philosophy.

By seeking to discover and stay in alignment with our own inner purpose, we can relinquish unnecessary negativity and the energy drain of competitiveness. Perhaps one of the greatest threats to successful achievement of any kind is the conscious or subconscious fear that someone else is more qualified, more important, or better connected than you. Since there is no one like you, and there is no one who can be you, there is no true competition.

The truth is, at this very moment, there are enough resources in this world for every man, woman, and child on Earth to be millionaires many times over.

In addition to the already existing wealth I have just mentioned, within the quantum field worlds of science, or the Omnipotent Invisible Supply of Divine Intelligence, there exist inexhaustible, untapped, and unlimited energy sources. Using this unlimited field for manifestation, creation, and fuel sources knows no bounds. Scientists know this and are currently in advanced stages of "fuel cell designs" and other technologies that will entirely transform our world economy, without negative costs to anyone except those who would accumulate wealth while sacrificing the well-being (and perhaps even the lives) of others.

Because of the Internet and other kinds of nonlocal communication, it is no longer possible for any entity, government, or group to suppress the incredible and vast treasures of information now being shared and implemented to create nonpolluting, opulent energy supplies and other methodologies of abundance.

If you are not already a millionaire, you can become one, and even more exciting, a contented millionaire, while creating and maintaining your inner foundation of *True Wealth*. Inner and outer wealth are not mutually exclusive, and in fact they create a healthy balance for one another. Monetary wealth without inner peace and *True Wealth* does not lead to life satisfaction. Conversely, the possession of *True Wealth* enables us to live through times of adversity with real life satisfaction. Millions of dollars have been lost and regained by those who maintain their inner *True Wealth* consciousness. They see their losses as temporary and inconvenient setbacks, rather than as devastating failures.

Sound Health, Sound Wealth

AUTHENTIC EMPOWERMENT

When we are authentically empowered, we are able to access and activate power from a source greater that our individual selves. By letting go of the often self-righteous power we feel when we operate at the lower frequencies of hate, judgment, unforgiveness, and feeling superior, we may actually become open and receptive channels for higher and better vibratory experiences. This is because our different emotional feeling states become electromagnetic messages that function as vibratory codes resonating to the long intertwined double helix of our very DNA. These electromagnetic messages resonate through the crystalline matrix of the molecules of our DNA. Frequencies, like triggers, activate different combinations of amino acids that become vibratory codes that function as chemical messengers to our bodies. This is the process through which we can move from low-frequency thoughts, feelings, and behaviors, into the higher-frequency thoughts, feelings, and behaviors of love, compassion, and empathy.

The human brain has the fluid capacity to recalibrate and reconfigure itself to a feeling-based thought.

In every moment, we are consciously and subconsciously making trillions of decisions that affect our health, well-being, quality of life, and longevity. We now have the power, the knowledge, and the means through which to change ourselves from lower frequencies into the higher frequencies. We can become more supple, more youthful, more loving and compassionate, more flexible, more successful, making better use of our deep intelligence and intuition.

Each and every thought and feeling we experience is either catabolic or anabolic in nature. This means the thought is either "life supporting" or "life destroying." The fact that you are alive and reading this and other related materials may indicate that you have had more life-supporting anabolic thoughts than catabolic destructive thoughts and feelings.

Thoughts, which are like "molecular votes," signal our bodies to create the corresponding biochemistry to support a particular thought or feeling. The intensity of the feeling amplifies the power of our thoughts and becomes manifest in our biology. Our thoughts magnetize experiences to us in both direct and mysterious ways.

Sound Health, Sound Wealth

Each and every choice, behavior, and thought we think either supports us as an organism or deconstructs us. Our thoughts (powered by our feelings) are the building blocks of the physical "temple of our beings." In addition to our inventory of where exactly our lives are today, we may powerfully correct and improve the "hard wiring" of our biology by overriding and reprogramming old effects through creating simple changes in our physiology.

I want tell to you about a very simple "powerful tool" for releasing the old neurochemistry that no longer serves you and installing new neurochemistry that serves you well. For example, if your mother or father, partner, or friend neglected you many times and you felt hurt, sad, resentful, afraid, helpless, and angry, you can imagine a container into which you put 90 percent of the painful thoughts and feelings, and in less than a second send the container down into the molten core of the Earth, where the feelings are already instantly transformed into energy that is useful and life-giving. After all, that is what Mother Earth does for us every millisecond of every day. You can fill this new space now available inside you with beautiful images, Technicolor dreams, all *Your Heart's Most Treasured Desires.*

Fortunately, we human beings are incredibly resilient, adaptive, and hardwired to move into healthy functioning. Our creative thoughts and beliefs can override our destructive and hopeless thoughts and feelings. Using our common sense assists us to do a nonjudgmental and honest assessment of how our feeling-based thoughts are contributing to our physical well-being or supporting a process of depletion.

Right now, in this very moment, we may build a new foundation from which we may resonate our "new lives," with enthusiasm and excitement, accelerating this process through the conscious use of our own physiology.

THE DECRYSTALLIZATION OF CONSCIOUSNESS

Deeply embedded psychological fears of separateness have led to competition, labeling, materialism, and the idealization of institutions, and have not led the human race to the peaceful paradise that almost all of us crave. When any perspective or social institution, such as capitalism, socialism, communism, democracy, fundamentalism, even New Age fundamentalism, theocracy, monarchy, oligarchy, totalitarianism, Nazism, particular religions of any kind, is forced upon others who don't want it, it becomes authoritarian, anti-life, and morally wrong. The stance that "You must believe the way I believe because I have 'special knowledge' that justifies my oppressing, suppressing, and controlling those who don't believe what I believe" is wrong and immoral, and inevitably leads to war and aggression.

When we acquiesce to the authoritarian stance and behavior of others, whether justified as "jihad" or "family values" in our personal relationships or in any other situation, we do so only out of fear, certainly not out of love. It happens, then, that thoughts, beliefs, ideas, and experiences become crystallized into our consciousness in ways that may keep us from realizing and enjoying our true "inner purpose."

This mental crystallization is caused by fear, and results in stereotyping, perceiving all "differentness" as threatening. Mental/emotional crystallization is limiting, constricting, even dangerous. It does not support diversity, creativity, basic human rights, or freedom.

In the same way, if our bodies produce a chronically unbalanced pH, that may cause filtrates to grow into crystals, which may result in a kidney stone, tumor, or other undesirable accumulations. Negative accumulations of any nature — physical, emotional, or Spiritual — can crystallize, creating blockages. Untoward thoughts and feelings may accumulate and crystallize, psychologically and emotionally, becoming like internal or external boulders, blocking essential pathways on the journey to fulfillment of *Your Heart's Most Treasured Desires.*

Sometimes, chronic ways in which we think and feel can, over time, become biological artifacts in the tissues of our bodies. Fortunately, the very flexibility of our emotions and our thoughts, as well as the cells that make up our tissues, may be remarkably restored when provided with the right resources.

Inner Wisdom, Purpose, and Grace

*"Let your life lightly dance on the edges of
time like dew on the tip of a leaf."*
– Rabindranath Tagore (1861-1941)

Our timeless "inner purpose" involves healing the "illusion of separateness" from our authentic selves, one another, other creatures, a blade of grass, a spectacular sunrise, or the vast starlit indigo sky — any person, place, and thing "out there." This healing experience seems to occur more frequently when we have steadfastly dedicated ourselves to a cherished purpose that enhances our own life and the lives of those around us. In such delightful moments of discovery, we know we are whole, complete, safe, connected, and Eternal.

Our internal world involves our relationship with Eternity, which is timeless. The more we feel connected and in harmony with our innermost selves, the more the moments of our lives are filled with increasing peace. We begin to feel safer, breathe more deeply and completely, and relax into the moment. We experience ourselves as an aspect of an Eternal Presence of Grace in this "Parenthesis in Eternity."

Because we live in physical bodies, our external world involves our ever-challenging relationship with time. We sometimes become confused about the meaning of our lives, how to balance our internal and external purposes in harmony. Our essential purpose in the world is often clouded when we feel pressured by internalized societal beliefs that we must be a certain way, feel a certain way, achieve certain things, in order to be accepted and acceptable. Each of us is "one of a kind," a unique individual essence that has existed from time immemorial, exists now, and will exist for all time. As long as we strive toward love, we are more than accepted, more than acceptable.

When we consciously attend to our inner world, our relationship with our Eternal self, and our connection to a greater whole, Divine Intelligence, the macrocosm of our external world just seems to magically Flow, naturally and creatively, often in unexpected and surprising ways. This is *Divine Flow*.

The ancient concept of Yin and Yang energies is expressed in our inner and external worlds, the microcosm and the macrocosm. Yin energy represents the feminine: alkalinity, nonviolence, patience, making others' needs a priority, calmness, the emotional, subjectivity, stability, peacemaking, and passivity. Yang energy represents the masculine: acidity, assertiveness and aggression, passion, impulsiveness, action, warrior stance, drives toward winning and success, objectivity, and intellect. Yin and Yang energies are all aspects of the same reality or phenomenon. We need both, but in appropriate balance to one another. Regardless of gender, our very human essence is neither Yin nor Yang, but instead a dance created by their union or quantum entanglement, within each of us, and among all of us.

For centuries, Yang energy has dominated our world of competitiveness and aggression. We have now arrived at a "choice point" in which we must balance these two energies by creating more Yin in both our inner and outer worlds.

From my heart to yours, I believe that we can individually and collectively create a new luxurious Earth, of peace, harmony, abundance, and bliss for all. We may each choose from the truth center of our hearts how we will fulfill our purpose, desire, and dreams. Although we are each unique as individuals, the bridging of science and Spirit have ultimately demonstrated that *We Are All One.*

"There are only two ways to live your life.
One is as though nothing is a miracle.
The other is as if everything is."
— Albert Einstein (1879-1955)

Sound Health, Sound Wealth

In the *Realm of the Miraculous*, We Are All One

I wish you Joy, Peace, Radiant Well-being,
Harmonious, Loving Relationships,
and all the Munificent Experiences you deserve.

Rich Blessings and Loving Regards,
Luanne Oakes, Ph.D.

As you apply the ideas in this book, you will certainly begin to manifest entirely new levels of health and abundance. I would love to continue to support you in this manifestation process for many years to come.

This is why I chose to create my website, www.soundhealthsoundwealth.com.

This website provides:

- A free e-newsletter with a personal message from myself each month, as well as my latest principles, strategies and tips for ongoing health and wealth.

- A "frequency treatment" room designed to accelerate the manifestation of *"Your Magical Divine Experiment*™*."*

- A Q&A section, where I answer your most important questions on how to apply the information in this book.

- Several other products and services, including my new lyrical CD *Seachange.*

Visit www.soundhealthsoundwealth.com today and sign up for my free e-newsletter!

Warmest regards,

Luanne

ABOUT THE AUTHOR

Luanne Oakes, Ph.D., is best known for her ability to successfully integrate Western and Eastern philosophies of science, spirituality, and health. With over 35 years' experience in the field of healing, with a wellspring of background in quantum physics, sound frequency, light, and color therapies, and the very latest research in science and technology, Luanne offers full-spectrum advanced healing techniques. Physicians, psychiatrists, psychologists, performers, and business professionals the world over have sought out her expertise, and have incorporated her healing practices into their lives with outstanding results. Her incredible system has been embraced and endorsed by such luminaries as Deepak Chopra, M.D. (author of *Ageless Body, Timeless Mind*), John Gray, Ph.D., (author of *Men Are from Mars, Women Are from Venus*), Anthony Robbins (author of *Awaken the Giant* and *Unlimited Power*), and Reverend Mary Murray Shelton (author of *Guidance from the Darkness*).